Straightforward Publishing
www.straightforwardco.co.uk

Straightforward Guides
Brighton BN2 4EG

© Straightforward Publishing 2008

ISBN 1847160 51 4
ISBN 13: 9781847160 51 5

Printed by Biddles Ltd Kings Lynn Norfolk

Cover design by Bookworks Islington

CONTENTS

3

INTRODUCTION

The main purpose of this book is to guide the reader through the maze of personal financial decisions which he or she or the family might have to make during a lifetime.

I have concentrated heavily on specific areas such as pensions, savings and insurance, because these are areas which will have the most effect on you during the course of your working life. The Book also discusses the operations of the stock market and how to invest wisely. There are also frequent references to financial advisors, ranging from the independent advisor to those employed by institutions such as banks. I have made repeated references because very often you will receive advice from such a person and will make decisions based on that advice.

As an individual, you could spend untold hours the various options open to you with regard to financial matters, only to find yourself more confused than ever due to conflicting advice received along the way. That advice will, quite often, be made in the best interests of the advisor, and his or her subsequent commissions, rather than in the best interests of yourself.

A Straightforward Guide to Personal Investments will set out, in a clear and unambiguous way, the meaning and implications of the various financial options open to you, and should leave you in a better position to make an informed choice.

The main areas covered by the book are mortgages, life insurance, savings, investments, income protection, stocks and shares, tax wills and trusts and pensions. In addition, I have covered education, health care, weddings and funerals.

Because of the importance of receiving accurate advice from financial advisors, the book will begin by outlining the law that governs such advisors and also the types of advice given.

Robert Stone 2008

Chapter 1

Financial Advice

There are many ways to purchase financial products nowadays, either through the Internet or by telephone. However, when considering more complex financial issues, it is evident that professional advice is needed. There are numerous advantages to using financial advisors, one of the main ones being that you will have extra protection if things go wrong. The first step towards finding a good advisor is considering which type is likely to provide the service you need. Like solicitors and other professionals, financial advisors do specialise and you would have to find the correct advisor for your needs. It is also very important to discover whether or not the advisor is properly authorised and registered and approved by the correct bodies. Nowadays, advisors and the companies that they work for must be authorised by the financial services watchdog, the Financial Services Authority (FSA). To be on the safe side you should always check with the FSA. You can also find out what type of business the advisor is authorised to do. These details are held on the FSA's register. Its public enquiries helpline is on 0845 606 1234. It is important to be aware of the distinctions between different types of advisors, the services they are likely to provide, and how they are likely to be paid, before narrowing your choice down.

Different types of advisers

Until recently, financial advisors were divided into two clear groups – tied and independent. The distinction was blurred by the introduction of multi-tied advisors to sell stakeholder pensions. Now the FSA is planning further changes in the way advisors are categorised. However, at present, the main categories of advisor are:

Tied

These individuals work for a particular company and can only sell you the products offered by that company. Employees of banks and insurance companies fall into this category. However, many small firms of self-employed financial consultants have the same status.

There is nothing wrong with buying financial products this way. Some of the lowest cost products are sold by tied agents. They also, however, sell some of the poorest value products. You should make your own comparisons of the value of their products and also of the charges and overall performance.

Multi-tied

This type of advisor acts as distributor for a limited range of companies. This will enable them to offer a choice of, for example, several different pension plans. However, again, they may not be the best available. You should ensure that you are seeing as wide a range as possible of products before making your choice.

Independent

These advisers can advise you on any company's products. They are required to make their recommendations based on the basic principles of 'best advice' and 'best execution'. This means that they should advise you which products are the best to meet your particular needs, and if there are a number of providers of these they should shop around to find best value. They do not have to recommend the cheapest product on the market if there are good reasons to recommend something else more suitable.

Qualifications and regulations

All financial advisers must have a level of qualification. To be registered, they must have passed the three levels of the Financial Planning Certificate (FPC) exam, or equivalent. The next stage for them is to take various levels of the Advanced Financial Planning Certificate (AFPC). Advisers who have passed ten subjects at AFPC level are regarded as among the best qualified.

Specialist advisers may have other relevant qualifications or be members of various professional bodies. Companies and advisers who are registered with the FSA must report regularly to the regulator and their affairs and business generally is inspected on a periodic basis by the regulators representatives. If a company or advisor does not meet the standards used to measure performance a fine can be imposed or an adviser's authorisation removed. The inspector can also tell the company to retrain their workforce.

Commission or fees

Advice from Financial Advisors does not generally come free. There are several ways in which a financial advisor can be paid.

Commission

Traditionally, most advisers have received commission for selling packaged financial products, such as insurance policies, pensions and savings plans. Although the financial institution offering the product pays the commission, this comes out of your money. The main advantage of this approach is that customers who do not have any capital can still obtain advice.

The commission-based approach has also had some very detrimental side effects. It has led unscrupulous advisors to recommend products because they paid high levels of commission rather than because they were the best choice for investor. This has been the main complaint against financial advisors in the past and has led to the industry being tightened up.

Another disadvantage with regular savings products, such as endowments or friendly society plans, is that the main part of the commission is often paid to the adviser as soon as the product is sold. As the amount of commission is often based on the term of the product, this meant large deductions being made initially sometimes absorbing the first few years' contributions. Although, by the end of the term the effect can be smoothed out, problems will arise if the saver stops paying into the contract for some reason.

Increasing regulation of financial advisors is helping to put an end to these practices. Nowadays, advisors have to provide key features documents when they sell investment products. Increasing regulation has meant greater transparency and more communication from advisor to client.

Fees

Some professional advisors, such as stockbrokers, accountants and solicitors have always charged fees. Under recent FSA proposals, financial advisors who want to call themselves 'independent' may be forced to do the same. The advantage of fees as opposed to commission is that the advisor is under no pressure to sell you any product at all and may be prepared to advise you about products that do not pay any commission.

For larger investors, paying fees can actually save money. Even though fee based advisors may charge upwards of £125 per hour, the final bill may still be less that commission based on a percentage of the amount invested.

Services offered by different advisers

Accountants

Accountants are usually the best source of advice on tax matters. Some can also advise on investments provided that they are authorised by the FSA. Some of the larger accountancy forms have specialist independent financial advice departments to provide a full planning service. You will have to pay a fee to accountants for such advice but any commission generated by sales of products is usually offset against the final bill.

For names of local accountants contact the Institute of Chartered Accountants, the Association of Chartered certified Accountants or the Chartered Institute of Taxation and Association of Tax Technicians (see appendix).

Actuaries

Actuaries are normally employed by insurance companies but there are also firms of independent consultants who can be approached for specialist advice on insurance related matter such as pension transfers. They work on a fee basis. The Association of Consulting Actuaries can provide you with the name of a firm in your area.

Banks and building societies

Most larger banks and building societies have in-house financial consultants who are tied agents. In the future, some banks may become multi-tied and start offering the products of several companies but their range will still remain limited. Some banks offer advice through private arms designed for wealthier customers (with more than £100,000 to invest for example).

Company representatives

Many insurance companies have their own sales forces to promote their products and services. Traditional insurers, such as Legal and General and the Co-operative still employ hundreds of representatives who will visit people in their own homes to discuss their needs.

Companies selling direct by telephone also use their own representatives.

Independent financial advisors

All IFA's can sell the products of any company in the market that they choose. However, there are considerable variations in the services they can offer. Some are small, often one-man operations, some belong to

17

national networks, and some are nationwide companies. Many are 'general practitioners' dealing mainly with packaged products, such as life insurance, pension products and unit trusts. Others offer more extensive financial planning whilst others specialise in particular areas, such as mortgages or investments. Although most IFA's are paid commission, many offer a choice nowadays and will work on a fee basis if clients prefer.

If you are looking for local, reputable financial advisers you can contact IFA promotion. For fee based independent advisers, contact the Money management Directory of fee based advisers. Organisations that promote professional development amongst their members are the Society of Financial Advisors (SOFA) and the Institute of Financial Planning. SOFA is the financial services arm of the Chartered Insurance Institute. It has three categories of membership depending on how many levels of the Advanced Planning Certificate (AFPC) advisors have achieved.

Solicitors

If you need legal advice on certain matters such as dealing with wills and probate, you will need to consult a firm of solicitors. They may also be able to provide financial planning and investment advice on a fee basis. There are two organisations that represent solicitors offering these services. They are the Association of Solicitor Investment Managers (ASIM) and Solicitors for Independent Investment Advice. If you have a legal problem relating to a pension, you should contact the Association of Pension Lawyers. See appendix for details.

Stockbrokers

Stockbrokers have become more accessible over the years, particularly recently. Many of the newer telephone based services cater mainly for investors who know which shares they want to buy and sell, and they do not provide advice other than general information bulletins. However, many firms still offer advisory and discretionary management services. For smaller investors, a unit or investment manage trust management may be offered.

To find out which stockbrokers offer these services to private clients, contact the Association of Private Client Investment Managers and Stockbrokers (APCIMS). It has a free directory of member firms, many of which provide a full financial planning service. See appendix for details.

Tied agents

Tied agents are also known as 'appointed representatives'. These are self-employed consultants or companies, which have a contract to sell one or more of an insurance company's products or commission. The agent may operate independently in respect of other business. For example, many building societies are tied agents and will sell the investment and investment products of one insurance company.

Complaints

If you are unhappy with a financial product or service, you have the means to complain. As with many complaints, you must first give the company the chance to put things right. If this cannot be achieved then there are other routes, such as the Financial Ombudsman Service.

However, before the Ombudsman will take up your complaint you must be able to show that you have followed the company complaint procedure and have still received no satisfactory solution to your problem.

Complaints schemes generally

The Financial Ombudsman Service. This provides a single complaints scheme divided into three specialist divisions for banking and loans, insurance and investments. It covers the following types of companies and organisations:

- Banks

- Building societies

- Financial advisors

- Firms dealing in futures and options/ Friendly Societies

- Fund managers

- Life insurance companies

- Pension providers

- Stockbrokers

The Office for the Pensions Advisory Service. OPAS provides initial advice and conciliation for complaints about employers pension schemes.

The Pensions Ombudsman. This ombudsman decides on complaints relating to employers pension schemes not resolved by OPAS.

The Mortgage Code Arbitration Scheme. This deals with complaints about mortgage intermediaries such as brokers and estate agents.

The General Insurance Standards Council. This is a voluntary scheme handling complaints about general insurance brokers such as those selling motor and household cover.

The Ombudsman for Estate agents. This is a voluntary scheme dealing with complaints about estate agents from both buyers and sellers. About a third of agencies are members.

Protection
If you lose money due to miss selling or misadministration, an ombudsman may be able to ensure that you get financial compensation. However, if fraud is apparent, this may not be possible, or if the company or individual becomes bankrupt.

The Financial Services Compensation Scheme

The maximum amounts of compensation are as follows:

- Deposits 100% of the first £2000 and 90% of the next £33,000 per individual (maximum £31,700)

- General Insurance Compulsory claims – 100%. Non-compulsory claims-100% of first £2000 and 90% of the rest.

- Long-term insurance 90% of the value of the policy, including future benefits.

- Investments 100% of the first £30,000 and 90% of the next £20,000. (maximum £48.000).

Pensions Compensation Board
This covers member liabilities of occupational pensions in full.

Offshore compensation

Investors should bear in mind that these schemes do not apply to firms based outside the United Kingdom. Although some offshore investment centres, such as the Isle of Man, may have their own compensation schemes, others do not. When investing outside the UK take great care to gain as much information as possible from the institution concerned.

Chapter 2

Mortgages

The options available

There comes a time in almost everyone's life when they need to leave the family home and establish their own independence. The majority cannot afford to buy a property immediately and so enter some form of rented accommodation, depending on circumstances. For those who wish to buy a property then the normal route is through obtaining a mortgage, unless you are fortunate to possess enough cash to purchase outright.

In recent years, the attitude of banks and building societies and other financial institutions has radically changed as they are all keen to lend you as much money as possible, subject to status (how much you earn)

In order to establish how much money you could borrow, the general criteria is as follows:

a) 2.5 x joint income;
b) 3 x higher income plus the lower income;
c) up to 3.5 x single income.

However, because of spiraling house prices, most lenders will lend more and some will lend over longer terms such as 35 years

Most building societies will lend a maximum of 95% of the purchase price of the property. It is important to remember that in order to gain a mortgage you must be credit worthy, have a steady or regular income and be confident in your ability to maintain such an important financial commitment.

Once you are aware of how much you can borrow, the difficult decision of deciding what type of mortgage you want has to be made. The options are many. However, there are a number of main ones which are outlined below:

The Variable Rate Mortgage
The Discounted Rate Mortgage
The Fixed Rate Mortgage
The Capped Rate Mortgage

The Deferred Rate Mortgage
Cashbacks
Interest Only

The variable rate mortgage is the most common, with the majority of borrowers preferring this type of loan. You will pay the rate of interest charged by the lender as standard and any increases or decreases in that rate will be reflected in your monthly payments.

Discounted Rate Mortgage
A discounted rate is usually offered by lenders to attract new business. They may offer a straight discount off the variable rate currently in force for a period of 1, 2 or 3 years after which time the rate of interest will simply revert to the standard interest rate at that particular time.

It is important to note that a discount of 1% for three years is 1% off the variable rate and therefore this will fluctuate as the variable rate changes.

Fixed Rate Mortgage
A fixed rate will guarantee that your mortgage payments will remain the same throughout the fixed rate period. After this time, your mortgage will simply revert to the standard variable rate. It is normal with any fixed rate that you will be charged a fee by the lender for the benefit of a fixed rate. It is always worth considering a fixed rate especially if the variable rate is low, as you will get a good rate of interest for a period of 2-10 years. With any fixed rate if you decide to sell your property within the fixed period you can be charged a redemption penalty, but most are portable and you can take the interest rate with you if you move property.

Capped rate mortgages
A capped rate mortgage means that your mortgage repayments may reduce below a certain level but will never go above that level during the capped rate period. This is very similar to a fixed rate but with the added advantage of the possibility of the payments going down. Once again, a fee is normally charged and redemption penalties are the same as the fixed rate.

Deferred Mortgages
A deferred mortgage is a very complicated means by which to repay a loan. Quite simply, it was very popular when rates were 15% and people

were struggling to maintain their payments. It is easier to explain with the illustration below:

Mortgage £100,000
Interest rate 8%
Deferred   25%
Mortgage repayments on interest only £666.66 (gross)
£40 tax relief
£626.66 total
-25% deferred
£156.67 x 12 = £1880.04 increase after one year
£469.99 net.

The difference gets compounded and added onto the loan, therefore after the deferral period, the mortgage balance has increased drastically and the mortgage payments could increase out of control. This type of mortgage is not recommended to anyone unless they expect a substantial change in income over a 3-5 year term.

Cash backs
In addition to all of the above mortgage options, most of the major lenders try to entice you to borrow from them by offering a cash incentive. For example, if you want a discounted rate, they may offer you a refund of your survey fee and possibly some additional money towards your legal expenses. If, however, you decided that you wanted to borrow at the normal rate of interest, some lenders may offer you a cash incentive of up to 7% of your advance. Like most other mortgages, you can find yourself penalised if you decide to transfer your mortgage in the earlier years.

Various methods of repayment
As if you did not have enough to think about, once you have decided on what mortgage you are going to have, it is now time to decide on how you are going to pay it back.

Traditionally, banks and building societies only lend money on the repayment method. However, with a change in the general wealth of the country and the significant increase in the number of people able to buy property, the industry quickly adopted new methods in order to meet the requirements of the individuals.

There are now five main types of repayments attached to mortgages:
Repayment

Endowment
Pension
ISA (Individual savings account)
Interest only

Repayment
When you borrow money on a repayment basis your repayments are made up of interest and capital, so that after each year you should see a slight reduction in the capital. After the 25-year period the mortgage is repaid and the property is owned outright.

Advantages of a repayment mortgage
If you intend to stay in the property for the full term you will be guaranteed to repay your loan. If you are approaching your late 40s and onwards, a repayment would probably be the cheapest option. You can also pay extra towards the mortgage to reduce the capital.

Disadvantages of a repayment mortgage
The interest is added onto the loan at the beginning so if you decide to move within the first ten years there will be no significant reduction in the capital. When you decide to move, the mortgage is not "portable" so you will have to start a further 25 years to reduce the term, but you will find the repayments a lot more expensive.

The Endowment mortgage
An endowment mortgage consists of two parts: the interest payable on the loan and premiums on the endowment. The purpose of the endowment is to grow, through regular contributions, to an extent where at the end of the mortgage term the value of the policy is sufficient to pay off the mortgage. If the insurance company has invested well you may receive a tax-free lump sum as well.

There are two main types of endowment: unit linked and low cost endowments. The main difference between the two can be attributed to risk and your attitude to that risk.

Low cost endowment
This is the traditional endowment which has been used to repay mortgages since endowments were introduced. The risk is moderate because your premiums are invested in low risk investments and each year

you receive a bonus which is added to your policy and cannot be taken away.

The bonuses are directly determined by the profit made by the company. At the end of the mortgage term the insurance company will give you a final bonus which will normally bring the value of the policy equal to, if not greater than, the mortgage.

As part of your endowment, you have life cover so that in the event of a fatality during the term of the policy, provided premiums have been maintained, a lump sum equivalent to the sum assured will be paid. Waiver of premium can be taken out as part of your endowment contract which would give you added protection in the event of not being able to work due to accident or sickness. The waiver benefit would pay your endowment premiums after 6 months of the claim and until such time as you would be able to return to your regular job.

Most endowment premiums remain constant throughout the term of the mortgage. There is however a low start endowment which would allow the cost of the endowment to drop significantly for the initial 3 or 4 years of the policy.

A new concept in the endowment range is the benefit of critical illness or serious illness protection. See life insurance further on in this book.

The unit-linked endowment
The purpose of the unit-linked endowment is exactly the same as the low cost endowment and that is to repay the mortgage at the end of the term. There are, however, fundamental differences in the way the money is invested, the bonus structure and the risk involved with this type of investment. The unit-linked endowment also has various additional contract options which are unique to the unit linked market.

How the money is invested
The Fund Managers will research the markets to establish where they can invest your money over the medium to long term in order to gain an investment return of above average performance. The investments can range from UK Securities to Overseas Quoted Equities, Fixed Interest, Property and Cash. As the scope for investment is so great it is important that you are always aware of the risk factors involved as they can vary quite drastically.

Bonus structure

The value of the policy is purely dependent on the value of the units in the various funds. Unit prices go up and down and therefore the value of the policy changes on a daily basis.

Additional benefits

Segmentation: A unit-linked endowment is written in clusters, normally ten and at any stage an individual part of the policy can be surrendered.

Early redemption: most endowments are expected to exceed the mortgage after 25 years, there is therefore the opportunity to redeem the mortgage earlier, should the value of the policy equal the mortgages.

Summary: the endowment method

Advantages

- Guaranteed life cover during mortgage term.
- The ability to continue your endowment regardless of how many moves and the ability to keep the term of the mortgages to 25 years.
- Option to build in financial protection in the form of waiver or critical illness.
- Low start options
- Early redemption option
- The potential of a tax free lump sum

Disadvantages

No guarantee that the mortgage will be repaid at end of term. The return is reliant on the investment of the relevant company. Endowments have been receiving a bad press in the last few years as many were miss sold policies and have found themselves in a position where the endowment has not performed well enough to provide enough capital to pay off the mortgage. Take very good advice indeed as to the nature of a particular endowment before entering into a deal.

Individual Savings Account mortgages

Once again, with this particular type of mortgage, you pay interest back to the lender and a premium to an insurance company or investment house. The premium is invested and hopefully at the end of the mortgage term the mortgage is repaid from the proceeds of the ISA.

Advantages of an ISA mortgage

- Tax efficiency
- Portable
- Can be used as a savings plan

Disadvantages

- No guarantee
- Can have extra cost of life cover
- No Waver of premium or critical illness allowed in ISA plan
- Limit of what can be invested

Pension Mortgages

The pension market is without doubt one of the most complicated areas of the financial services industry.

Pension mortgages are mainly targeted at people who are not able to take advantage of an occupational pension scheme and those who are self employed. Pension mortgages can be offered to people who are employed but it is generally considered best advice to take advantage of the company pension scheme therefore making a pension mortgage an unlikely option.

Considerations

The mortgage cannot represent any more than 25% of the total pension fund at the expected retirement age. The reason for this is that on maturity the maximum cash sum available from the pension is 25% of the fund and the remainder is to provide a pension.

If you are likely to consider the advantages of a pension mortgage you must be able to protect your likely future income and job career prospects as you will be expected to maintain a high level of pension contributions throughout the mortgage term.

To protect the mortgage debt, you will be expected to take out term assurance in order to secure the loan amount for the benefit of the lender.

If you expect your career to change from self-employed to employed with the prospect of a company pension it is generally considered that a pension mortgage would not be suitable for your future requirements.

Advantages of a pension mortgage
- Provides a pension and repays mortgage.
- Tax relief on contributions.

- The pension fund is non-taxable.

Disadvantages

- Early retirement option purely dependent on the performance of the pension fund.
- A pension mortgage would normally be more expensive than a standard repayment or an endowment mortgage.
- A great deal of the pension is in order to pay off the mortgage
.

A pension cannot be in joint names.

Interest only mortgages

An interest only mortgage can be compared to having an endowment mortgage without the endowment. Quite simply, the capital will not increase or decrease provided interest payments are maintained. This type of loan is often used for short-term finance or in special cases where individuals cannot afford to cover the costs of capital and interest mortgage.

Advantages of interest only mortgages

- Cheap mortgage.
- This method is quite often used by pensioners who want to release capital from their homes to provide them with a lump sum.

Disadvantages

- The term could be endless. The debt never reduces unless paid off.

Associated costs of buying a property

It is important to establish the likely expenditure you will be expected to make before completion of a transaction.

Before a bank or building society will make you an offer they will insist on carrying out a valuation of the proposed property to ensure the property represents adequate security for them to be able to advance you the mortgage monies. The valuation or survey is paid by you and the cost differs from lender to lender. There is also a choice of what type of report you can have carried out in addition to the basic valuation.

Listed below is a general idea of the costs for the various surveys for the purchase of a house costing £275,000:

Valuation for mortgage purposes - £475
Report on condition and valuation - £480
Structural Survey - £500

From time to time a number of mortgage lenders offer free valuations when you apply for a mortgage through them. If you are considering a fixed rate mortgage you will normally be expected to pay a fee. This fee will range from £50-£395 and is paid in most cases on application. Before paying this fee you should find out whether this money is refundable should the transaction not proceed, as in most cases the lender will not return payment.

Mortgage indemnity or guarantee premium

Whenever banks or building societies lend more than 75% of the value of the property they insure themselves in the event of future loss in the form of mortgage indemnity. This policy is purely for the benefit of the lender, the premium however is payable by you the applicant. The bigger the deposit you can put down the less indemnity you will pay. Some lenders will allow you to add the indemnity to the mortgage.

Please note that some lenders now pay the MIGP for purchasers up to 90% loan to value and some lenders pay the MIGP up to 95%.

Solicitors' fees

A solicitor has to be appointed to act on your behalf and also of the relevant lender. All lenders have a panel of acceptable solicitors and you should check to make sure that you are using a firm that is acceptable otherwise you could be expected to pay two sets of fees.

Your solicitor will carry out various checks and searches and will make numerous enquiries with the owner's solicitors about any issues you or the lender may need to have clarified before you commit yourself.

Based on a purchase price of £275,000 the fees payable to your solicitor would be approximately: £2000 approx plus vat inclusive of disbursements but excluding stamp duty.

Illustration of Solicitors' Fees and Disbursements

Purchase price   £275,000

Legal fees:
Solicitors   £400 + vat
Stamp Duty   £8250 (3%)
Local Authority search fee   £180 approx.
Land Registry fee   £140 approx.
Land Registry search fee £5
Bankruptcy search fee   £1 per client
Other searches such as contamination and water and sewerage etc £200

The most important part of the initial cost is, of course, the deposit money. You will normally be expected to provide at least 5% deposit. This money must be from your own savings or a gift from family etc. because if you are borrowing the money it is effectively a 100% loan. The deposit money is paid to your solicitor on exchange of contracts as this is the time of the transaction when you totally commit yourself to the property. You would normally move in two or three weeks after.

Chapter 3

Life Insurance

The concept of life insurance is by no means a 20th century development. The earliest forms can be traced back to Greek and Roman times. Clubs would be formed and, for a regular contribution, a lump sum would be paid in the event of death of an individual.

In today's society, we are expected to insure for virtually everything and anything and at the end of the month there are normally limited funds to insure for the most important issue, YOU.

Do you need it?

Many people feel they do not need life insurance. In some cases this is true but the vast majority have families and feel that they need to be protected in the event of an unexpected death. It is not always the main income provider who needs all the life cover. Provisions must be made if there are children and the non-working parent spends his or her time looking after them. The cost of employing a child minder or even giving up your full time job must be considered. This could be easily remedied with a basic life insurance policy.

If you have a mortgage the banks and building societies normally insist that you have the relevant life insurance to cover the mortgage debt and in the case of endowment mortgages the life insurance forms part of your endowment premiums, but with repayment mortgages the cost of premiums is extra.

As you are probably aware, if you haven't got any life cover other than in conjunction with your mortgage then you are likely to be under-insured.

If you are in an occupational pension scheme you are likely to have cover as part of your benefits. This would normally work out to be 3 times your basic salary and if you have a personal pension plan you can have life cover up to 3 times and you would receive tax relief on your premiums.

To establish how much life cover you require you need to calculate how much income the family needs to survive each year. Take away any state benefits you would be or are entitled to and then multiply this figure by the number of years your youngest child has before he or she leaves school.

Example

A family requires £15,000 per year income.

No benefits available.

The youngest child is 9. Therefore there is a minimum of 7 years before the child could leave school and start work.

7 x 15 = £105,000 life cover

You could say that the life cover quoted would be too much after the first year, but the youngest child could always go on to sixth form or college and may not actually start work until he or she is 20 years old.

Different types of life insurance

Most forms of life insurance are paid on a monthly or yearly premium basis. The premium you pay will purchase a level of cover and it can be on a fixed or variable term. There are a multitude of insurance policies geared to the individual's needs and requirements, and we will now look at the differences.

Decreasing Term Assurance

This policy is commonly known as mortgage protection and is normally used in conjunction with a repayment mortgage. As we have already discovered with a repayment mortgage the debt reduces further throughout the term and the same can be said about the decreasing term insurance. The amount of life cover will decrease in line with the mortgage. This policy can be written in joint names and is the cheapest form of life assurance available. There is no investment value to this contract and in the event of a claim, the benefits are payable to the estate.

Example

Mortgage Protection Assurance

Male non-smoker age at entry not exceeding 30

Female non-smoker age at entry not exceeding 30

Benefits

Initial sum assured	£50,000
Plan Term	25 years

Monthly cost

Premium payable for 25 years

or until first death if earlier   £9.57

Warning - the contract has no cash-in value at any time.

Level term insurance

This policy works on the same basis as the above, but the life cover will not reduce as the term goes on. For this reason, the premiums are slightly more expensive.

Family income benefit policy

This policy will simply provide an annual income for your dependents instead of a lump sum. This is a good way too ensure that the provisions that you have made are not used up in one spending spree.

Once again, this contract can be written in joint names, but has no investment value.

Whole life

This type of policy is considered to be the most flexible contract in the life insurance market. Unlike the other contracts this policy does have investment value and it is not written on a fixed term. The amount of cover you require can be altered at any time to suit changes in your personal circumstances. The premiums you pay are not fixed and are reviewed every 5-10 years to establish whether the insurance cover can still offer you the level of cover for the premium you are paying.

This policy is quite expensive in comparison to term policies. It is, however a great deal more flexible and it can be written in joint names.

Example
Whole of Life min/max cover basis

Male, non-smoker, age 30 next birthday

Female, non-smoker, age 30 next birthday

Amount of Life Cover payable on first death:

minimum   £10,350

maximum   £114,900

Monthly premium   £25

Critical illness

A new innovation in the insurance industry is the introduction of critical illness insurance.

Surveys have shown that more people are concerned about being diagnosed as having a critical illness than they are of dying. The implications of having a major illness are immense as you could find yourself stuck with the financial commitments but without the income and ability to pay them. The introduction of critical illness means that if you are diagnosed with any of the defined illnesses in the contract, you will receive a lump sum. The amount of the lump sum depends on your premiums and your age. The benefit of critical illness means that you can afford private medical treatment or afford to pay off your debts. Below are listed the main conditions that are considered to be critical illness:

-multiple Sclerosis--heart attack--kidney failure--loss of a limb
-stroke--major organ transplant—cancer—Coma--benign brain tumour
-severe burns

This is not a technical guide or a total list of definitions. It is simply a selection of some definitions. Critical illness can be taken out by itself, or as part of a whole life or endowment. Critical illness does not have investment value. It can be written in joint names.

Example
Male, non-smoker, age next 30 next birthday
Female, non-smoker, age 30 next birthday
Initial monthly premium £25.00
Initial sum assured   £65,000
Life Assured basis   joint life, first event
Cover type   Maximum

The premium is payable until the earlier of the:
- death of the last to die of the lives assured.
- diagnosis of one of the lives assured suffering a critical illness.

The premium will increase annually by the amount required to support the increase in benefits as a result of the Automatic Increase Option.

What the benefits might be
The greater of the sum assured and the encashment value of the plan will be payable on the diagnosis of one of the lives assured suffering a critical illness.

Chapter 4

Savings

People save for a number of different reasons, dependent on their circumstances and on age. Some people save in order to have enough to help their children and others save for a prosperous old age. Whatever the reason, it is important to understand the best vehicles for savings

Those skilled in the art of financial planning consider that a sum of between three and six months expenditure constitutes an adequate fund for emergencies. This will depend on your employment status as if you are self-employed then you may need more due to the fact that you will not get sick pay unless you are insured.

This emergency cash should be placed in an account that is readily accessible, probably in an instant access account which allows you to withdraw without penalty. However, these accounts traditionally pay the lowest form of interest and it is advisable to shop around.

There are a number of newer accounts, such as telephone only accounts which offer a higher rate of interest with instant access. You are provided with a card so that you can gain access to your money as and when you need it. If the account is joint, then both partners should be provided with a card. In addition to phone accounts there are internet accounts. Although some of the providers are large established institutions such as Northern Rock and Abbey National, some are smaller companies with far less capital. You should always think before investing with any company. Think about your needs and requirements and the security of your capital.

Cash returns

A lot of savers like to have more cash on deposit than they need for emergencies. If you do not need access to the money for emergencies then it is better to put your money in a higher rate account, one which generally needs notice of withdrawal. The longer the period of notice the more interest that you will get on your money.

Postal accounts also pay higher than standard rates of interest and these are useful for those savers who do not require access to their savings over a foreseeable period.

You can get an idea of interest rates by perusing the pages of the dailies and weekend editions of papers, which compare the costs of borrowing and returns on savings. In the United Kingdom rates for deposits are usually quoted gross of tax. Rates may be quotes on two different bases.

The nominal rate is the rate of interest applied to the account, while the annual effective rate (AER) is the rate taking into account the frequency of interest payments.

The nominal rate is not affected by whether you draw your interest or leave it in the account. But if interest is paid more than once a year and you leave it there, you will earn interest in interest and end the year with more in your account.

The table below shows the difference between the nominal and effective rates depending on how often interest is credited to your account.

If you plan to spend all your interest, you can compare different accounts on the basis of their nominal interest rates. If you plan to leave the interest to accumulate, as the table shows, an account with a lower nominal interest rate could give you a better deal if it is credited more frequently. In this case, you should use the annual effective rate as a comparison.

Annual effective rate if interest is credited

Yearly	Half-yearly	Quarterly	Monthly	Daily
Nominal rate				
5%	5%	5%	5.09	5.12%
5.13%				
8%	8%	8.16%	8.24%	8.30%
8.33%				

Tax on interest earned

Tax is usually deducted at source in interest paid. This is a requirement of the effective legislation. Tax is deducted at 20%. If you pay a lesser rate of tax then you can reclaim overpaid tax. To have interest on savings paid without deduction of tax, the account holder has to sign a form R85 declaring that you are a non-taxpayer. Parents can sign this on behalf of children. If the interest paid to a child from money given to it by parents is over £10 then this will be taxed as if this were the parent's income.

Banks based outside the UK, i.e. offshore are not subject to UK tax legislation and many of these institutions offer interest gross. Whether you receive it gross or not you are still obliged by law to declare it on your tax return. It is the savers responsibility to declare the tax.

Some National Savings accounts pay interest gross and this is subject to the same rules, i.e. the taxpayer declaring the interest received.

The choice of accounts

There are a wide variety of accounts available from banks and building societies. Many accounts have differing features. Most pay variable interest but some pay fixed rates. The following are some of the accounts on offer.

Children's accounts

These accounts sometimes offer better variable rates than can be gained on a small deposit on a regular savings account. These accounts can also offer free gifts for children, such as magazines, moneyboxes etc.

Instant access accounts

These permit withdrawal of capital without notice, though there is usually a restriction on how much cash can be withdrawn on one day. The interest rate is variable. Interest may be credited yearly, half yearly, quarterly, monthly or daily. With most accounts, the rate will depend on the amount invested.

Internet accounts

These accounts can only be set up over the internet. The initial transfer is made from your current account, as are future transfers. Interest rates are usually higher than traditional accounts.

Mini-Isas

The individual savings account takes two forms, the mini-isas and the maxi-isas. A mini-isa can contain cash, equities (stocks and shares) or insurance, while a maxi-isa can contain all three elements.

You can take out a mini-isa of each kind each year or a single maxi-isa, but you cannot invest in both in a single tax year. You can invest up to £3000 per year and these isas are tax-free.

The maximum for a maxi-isa is £7000 in a single tax year.

These rules are subject to change so you should check with your bank or building society.

Monthly income accounts

These types of accounts may have a minimum notice period for withdrawal. The income is usually paid direct to your current account and there is usually a £250 minimum amount.

Notice accounts

Money can be withdrawn without penalty by giving the appropriate amount of notice. If you withdraw without notice you will lose interest on the amount you would have been paid during the notice period. There is usually a minimum deposit of £1000 or more.

Postal accounts

Some building societies offer these accounts, where deposits and withdrawals can only be made by post. Interest rates are variable and may be higher than on instant access accounts, as are the minimum investments required.

Telephone accounts

The initial deposit is made by cheque. You set up a direct debit arrangement on your current account and can then transfer money between it and your telephone account. You have to set up a security code and cite this when calling to transact business. Interest rates are usually very competitive.

Time deposits

The interest rate is fixed for the time of the deposit, often 30 days onwards. There will be a penalty for early withdrawal. Interest is usually added at the end of the period that is fixed and is usually gross of tax.

Fixed-rate investments

You can commit your money for a fixed period; say five years, at a certain rate of interest, say 6%. If rates are at 4% this may seem attractive but rates can rise during the period. Before investing for the longer term at fixed rates you should consider carefully the market in the longer term and decide whether you want to make this gamble. Fixed interest rates will offer you a reasonable return over the period and it is difficult to predict interest rates over the longer term.

Short-term fixed-rate investments-Escalator bonds

These are issued by building societies and pay a rate of interest that rises each year for a fixed period. Since these are fixed rate accounts you cannot get it back early or there can be a significant financial penalty. You should always think about the consequences of your wish to invest in this type of product.

Fixed rate bonds

These accounts pay a flat fixed rate of interest for a fixed period from one to five years. Early withdrawal is not usually permitted without a penalty. There will be a minimum investment.

Guaranteed growth bonds

Issued by insurance companies, these guarantee a fixed rate for a specified period, usually between two and five years. A lump sum is paid at the end of the term. The return is treated as having borne basic rate tax so there will only be an additional liability if you are a higher rate taxpayer.

Guaranteed income bonds

These pay a fixed income for a specified term, usually two to five years. The tax treatment is the same as for the above bonds.

Maxi-isas

Some companies offer maxi-isas for a fixed rate of return for periods of up to five years. Sometimes a rate of income is guaranteed but you may not get all your capital back unless a stock market index (FTSE100 usually) is above a certain level. These are higher-risk so careful thought needs to go into investments such as this.

National Savings Certificates

These grow in value at a fixed rate for a period of up to five years. The profits are exempt from tax and there are limits on how much you can invest.

National Savings Pensioners Guaranteed Bonds

These pay a fixed amount of income over two to five years. The interest is taxable but is paid without deduction at source.

Longer-term savings plans
Isa savings plans

Maxi-isas, in which you may invest or save up to £7000 each tax year up to 5th April 2008, are well suited to regular savers. They are exempt from income tax and capital gains tax. They give access to a range of investment funds and offer flexibility. Minimum savings are usually £50-100 per month. There is a cost of between 1% and 5% of each contribution within the year plus an annual charge on the assets of the fund of between 0.5% and 2%. Look at the charges carefully. Isas must be in the name of one individual. You cannot take out a maxi-isa in a child's name.

Unit trust savings plans

Unit trusts and open-ended investment companies are similar in having a pool of money which they manage on behalf of individual and corporate investors. The pool expands or contracts depending on the additions or withdrawals into it and the value of a unit or share is the value of the investments in the pool divided by the number of units or shares in issue. A wide variety of funds are available, investing in a variety of areas and countries. Minimum monthly savings are from £30-£50. The income received is taxable and will usually be taxed at source. Higher rate taxpayers will receive a certificate showing what they have paid at source and they will be personally responsible for any extra payments. Costs vary from 1%-5% of each contribution with an annual charge of 0.5% to 2% of the value of your assets. You can take out a plan in the name of a child.

Investment trusts

Unlike unit trusts or open-ended investment companies, investment trusts do not issue new shares to savers but buy existing shares through the stock market. This is because investment trusts have a fixed pool of assets and the price of a share in the market may be higher or lower than its net asset value. These schemes are rum by investment trust managers. They usually subsidise the costs of the plan, which are much lower than the costs of buying investment trust shares through a stockbroker. The annual charges are between 0.5% and 2%. The taxation rules and child rules are the same as for unit trusts.

With profits savings plans

With profits savings plans are in the form of endowment polices issued by insurance companies. Though they are life policies, they provide very little life cover. Most of the premiums that are paid are used to invest in the companies with profits fund, which is a giant pool of assets usually worth billions of pounds. The fund will hold a variety of assets including fixed rate investments, UK and overseas shares and property.

The with-profits policy has a sum assured, which is the minimum amount that is paid on death or at the maturity rate. Two types of bonus are added to the sum assured. Reversionary bonuses are added each year, often at quite a lower rate of 3% or so. At maturity (or death) a terminal bonus is added which can be equal to al the reversionary bonuses paid. Once a reversionary bonus has been added to a policy, it cannot be taken away, but terminal bonus rates are not guaranteed and can be varied at any time. With-profits policies are of two types. Some have one fixed maturity date, while with a 'flexible policy' you can en-cash it at several different dates, usually at five-year intervals. The charges for with profits policies are typically about 12-15% of premiums over the term. The term for these policies is usually quite long, being anything from 10-25 years so careful thought needs to be given to this type of investment. They are only really suitable if you can sustain your savings over this long period.

Friendly society plans
Friendly societies are permitted to run tax-free savings schemes with low minimum and maximum investments. Some are of the with-profit types, while others are unit-linked. The plans have a minimum term of ten years and the high costs can wipe out other benefits so again careful thought has to be given to this type of investment.

The purpose of saving
The purposes of saving, as we have seen, are many and will differ depending on your circumstances and long-term view. Some of the more usual savings objectives are to provide retirement income, to pay for children's education (see later) to reduce debt such as mortgage and for general purposes, for life's little luxuries. Whatever you choose, you should do so carefully, think about the short and long-term advantages and don't take unnecessary risks.

Chapter 5

Single Premium and Lump Sum Investments

If you are able to consider investing a lump sum of money, you must take great care in establishing your requirements for that investment and also your own future plans. For example:

-you may not be worried about getting a significant return as long as it is likely to better the return you would get from your building society account;

-you need the best return possible over the next five years without jeopardizing capital;

-you aren't worried how the money is invested provided you don't receive a tax bill;

Quite clearly, the important issues to remember when investing a lump sum are:

1. the amount of money you can afford to invest;
2. the term of the investment;
3. the risk involved with the investment;
4. tax implications.

As we have already seen in the regular savings chapter, there are numerous ways in which you can invest your money and the same considerations should be made whether you are saving on a regular basis or a lump sum.

The options available
Your choice of investment will obviously depend on your own personal financial circumstances. Below you will find details of the most popular investments currently available.

High interest building society accounts

If you are concerned about the risk attached with investing your money, then you cannot do a lot better than your building society. Although some people may consider investing in their building society as unattractive, you haven't got any worries about how your money is being invested. For lump sums, building societies often offer a wide range of higher rate accounts with a tiered rate of interest, depending on the size of investment.

Most high rate accounts have a notice period which must be given for any withdrawals. This may not apply, however, if the balance of the account remains over £5,000. A large number of high rate accounts will allow you to take a regular income on a monthly basis. The interest received on these accounts has already been taxed at a composite rate and should you be a high rate tax-payer, you may have a tax liability on the interest.

National savings

Most national savings are calculated gross and therefore you would have a tax liability if you are a tax payer, therefore reducing the benefit of investing. There are however, a limited number of savings opportunities that deserve a mention.

Ordinary accounts

This is a basic account which will allow you to invest between £10-£10,000. The interest rate increases for amounts in excess of £500. This is a good investment for higher rate tax-payers as the first £70 interest is non-taxable.

Savings certificates

This is a good way of investing your money over a five-year period especially if interest rates are high. The interest you will receive is fixed and tax-free and you can invest a maximum of £10,000 or £20,000 if you re-invest after the first five years.

Indexed linked certificates

These certificates are based on the rate of inflation and on the five- year term of the savings certificates. If inflation looks like it is going to constantly increase, this is a very attractive investment for minimum risk as you will receive a tax-free bonus after 5 years.

Investment bonds

Investment bonds are considered a medium to long-term investment and the investment options range from the with profits investments to investments in the property markets and overseas. The risk is always a major factor in any investment and you should be aware exactly where your money is being invested and the relative risk.

All major insurance companies offer investment bonds and they can be used for both capital growth and income if required. The investment fund is taxable and payments are made net of basic rate tax. There is an allowance however, which will allow both basic rate and higher rate taxpayers to withdraw up to 5% of the fund value each year without liability.

The minimum amount that you can invest in a bond is normally £2,000 and you should consider investing it for a minimum of five years. In the case of an emergency, you would be able to gain access to your money but the value will relate to the period of investment, charges and market conditions.

The main points to remember are that you should invest in a bond that suits your attitude to risk. If you are a higher rate taxpayer you may be able to reduce any liability if you can cash in the bond when the income drops to the basic rate bracket.

Guaranteed Capital Investments

This is a relatively new concept in the insurance industry as your investment is directly linked to the performance of the FTSE one hundred. If you read the financial press or watch the main television news you will always see a reference to the FTSE one hundred. It provides a clear indication of how the stock market is behaving as it monitors the share prices of the top 100 companies in the UK.

From day to day the prices of each company's shares can change for any reason and towards the bottom of the index the smaller companies are constantly competing to secure their position within the top 100.

The growth of the FTSE is often compared to that of banks and building societies (see single premium investments) and over a long term period is considered to be a valuable alternative to the standard options. Traditionally, the FTSE has outperformed the returns offered by building society accounts and for that reason most insurance companies will guarantee that on completion of the five year term you will at least receive your original investment, thereby reducing the risk factor.

The minimum investment is usually £6,000 and the fund and benefits are paid net of basic rate tax. Guaranteed capital investments are offered on limited availability and are not able to provide an income. They are, however, a worthwhile consideration when you are building up an investment portfolio.

Unit Trusts

The purpose of the unit trust is to give individuals the opportunity to invest directly in the stock market. There are a multitude of investment opportunities ranging from UK equities to shares in Japan and North America. In order to overcome the charges and realise a profit, you must look at investing your money in a unit trust for at least three years or longer.

Unit trusts can be used for capital growth or income and you should obtain help from a financial advisor to choose the most suitable trust for your performance. Once you have chosen your trust and paid your money, you will be issued with a certificate. It is very important that you keep this in a safe place as you will need to produce it when you cash it in.

To establish how well your investment is doing, you can phone the trust managers or look at the share page of any quality newspaper. You will normally see two columns, the offer price and the bid price. For the purpose of selling you must multiply the bid price by the number of units you hold.

The tax implications

Unless you are a higher rate tax-payer it is unlikely that you will have any tax liability on the income or gain of the investment. If you are a higher rate tax-payer there are various ways of mitigating your liability and you should discuss this with a financial advisor before committing yourself to any investment.

Individual Savings Accounts

We have already looked at ISA's in depth. ISA's, as they are known have been made available since April 5th 1999 when PEP's and TESSA's were withdrawn. Refer to pages 50-51 for a detailed breakdown of ISA's.

Chapter 6

Income Protection

We all realise the importance of life insurance. We do however mainly neglect the need to ensure that there is adequate protection to cover accidents or illness that prevent us from working and therefore maintaining our normal standard of living.

Most employers restrict the length of time that they will make full payment to the employee in the event of illness and the self employed are likely to receive even less.

To protect against accident or sickness, you can take out an income protection plan. For a monthly premium you can cover a pre-determined amount of money relative to a maximum two thirds of your income. The premium you will pay will depend on:

1. How much benefit you require;
2. Your age;
3. How long you are prepared to wait before you receive benefits (deferment period 4 weeks - one year);
4. Your medical condition;
5. Your occupation.

If you make a claim on your income protection policy, the benefits will be paid to you until such time as you are able to return to your normal job or one of a similar nature, or your expected retirement date. This type of cover will not protect you against redundancy.

In the event of a claim, the benefits you receive represent and replace your income and therefore attract tax at the relevant rate.

Cover offered by banks and building societies
The threat of losing your job is common in today's society and it is something that could ruin your lifestyle and bring great hardship to you and your family.

The banks and building societies are of course aware of this and therefore offer you the opportunity to apply for a scheme which will protect you and your partner (in the case of a joint mortgage) against accident or sickness or involuntary redundancy. This is sometimes referred to as mortgage payment protection or payment care.

The premiums for these types of schemes range from £6 per £100 of cover to £9 per £100. A claim can only be made and benefits paid once you have been unable to work for a period of three months, after which stage the benefits are normally paid for a period of one to two years for sickness and also for redundancy. Some insurers when paying benefit will send a cheque direct to your lender each month to ensure you are using the money for the purpose that was intended.

These schemes have proved very popular and you should seek further information about them from the relevant lender, as you are not likely to be given a chance to take out a policy after your mortgage has been completed.

You can also allow for extra benefit from these policies to cover the cost of any endowments or life insurances that may run in conjunction with the mortgage.

This type of cover is of benefit to the employed but the redundancy cover is obviously of no benefit to the self-employed and a good permanent health insurance would be more relevant. If the benefits of the scheme are paid direct to you, that would constitute income and income tax would be payable at the relevant rate.

Chapter 7

Tax

Income Tax

Regardless of whether we are employed or self-employed, we all have to accept the fact that the Inland Revenue are going to take a percentage of our income in the form of income tax and there is nothing we can do to avoid it.

The employed and self-employed are treated in slightly different ways and therefore we shall look at each individually, once we have assessed the structure of income tax. You should check your current tax allowances with the Inland Revenue as they are subject to annual change.

Income Tax Structure

All people under 65
Tax allowance £6305
65-74 £7550
75 and over £7690

The personal allowance shows how much a person can earn before they have to pay any tax. In the case of a married man he can earn slightly more before paying tax. (The married person's allowance, however, can be transferred to the spouse if requested.)

The first £2230 of a persons income is taxable at 10%. From £2231 to £34600 @22% from £34601 @40%. (tax year 2007-2008)

The various rates of tax are called the marginal rates.

The Employed

If you are employed your tax affairs are conducted on the fiscal year or financial year which is 6th April to 5th April the following year.

You are taxed on what is known as Schedule E (Pay As You Earn) which means that both tax and national insurance will be deducted by your employer before you receive your salary cheque. You therefore receive your salary net of tax. This is without doubt the simplest way to conduct your tax affairs as there is very little further communication you need to have, if any, with your tax office.

At the end of the financial year you will receive a P60 which is a statement of your full year's earnings and it will contain details of how much tax and national insurance you have paid as well as pension contributions if you are in an occupational pension scheme.

You should always keep your P60 in a safe place as it often requested by banks and building societies for mortgage or loan purposes.

If you work for a large employer you may receive fringe benefits such as a company car, mortgage subsidy, or private medical insurance. These are very worthwhile benefits but you must remember they are also taxable benefits which will mean that your personal allowance will reduce to account for the real value of these benefits. If you have such benefits but notice your tax code hasn't changed then it is your responsibility to inform your tax office, as failure to do so may mean that in future years they could claim payment for undisclosed benefits.

Not all benefits are taxable, however, and the most attractive one is obviously a company pension scheme. In recent years a great deal of companies have moved towards Performance Related Pay and there is a tax concession which will allow them to pay a bonus known as Profit Related Pay up to a maximum of £4000 pa without any tax liability regardless of your marginal rate. This is obviously an excellent concession for everyone concerned. Employees who earn less than £8500 receive lenient treatment with regard to the cost of any benefits they receive.

When you leave employment you will be provided with a P45 which is similar to a P60 but is for the benefit of your new employer to use in order to calculate your earnings to date and therefore make the necessary stoppages in your salary. It is always worthwhile taking a copy of your P45 for your own reference.

The self-employed

If you are self employed your own tax year can be any period of 12 months you want. In the eyes of the Inland Revenue you will be taxed on what is known as Schedule D and pay Class 2 National Insurance contributions.

Being self employed means that the money you receive for the services you provide will be gross and therefore no tax will have been deducted.

It is advisable that you keep an accurate record of all the money you receive and receipts for any money you spend in connection with your business activities. At the beginning of April you would normally receive a tax return form which explores all the potential sources of income you may have. This must be duly signed and returned within a month.

A large percentage of the self employed use the services of an accountant, as they best know the ways in which your tax liability can be reduced and their services certainly make it easier if you are self-employed and are hoping to take out a mortgage.

The Inland Revenue will negotiate with you or your accountant once they have details of your year's earnings and business expenses. Once the expenses have been taken from the gross figure this will leave your net income and therefore the amount upon which you will be expected to pay tax.

Your tax liability is normally paid in 2 installments, the first on 1st January and the second on the 1st July. The Inland Revenue, however, do not wait for your accounts to be completed and in most cases you will be expected to make installments based on assessments of your expected income and once your accounts are finalised you will then be informed of any over or under payment.

Capital Gains Tax

If you have successfully bought and sold investments, antiques and property etc., you may find that you would be liable for capital gains tax.

Everyone is allowed to make a profit on opportunities that they fund with their own capital. There is, however, a limit, which you should check with the Inland Revenue, and any profit/gain that exceeds that figure would be liable for capital gains tax at the individual's marginal rate.

Inheritance Tax

The subject of death is one which is rarely discussed openly and inheritance tax is thought to be an issue that is largely limited to the wealthy. This however, is a misconception, as inheritance tax will affect more people now than ever before. In order to establish whether you are going to have an inheritance tax bill, you must assess the total value of the estate left by the deceased. This would include all assets and any gifts made within the preceding seven years. If the total figure exceeds £300,000 (2007-8) there will be a liability on the surplus of 40%. If the estate totals less than £300,000 there will be no liability. You should check these limits with the Inland Revenue as they are subject to change.

It now becomes clear that if you have been able to build a reasonable amount of savings, paid off your mortgage and may have received a pension lump sum and an inheritance yourself, you could be bordering on the £300,000 limit and your estate would be liable for inheritance tax.

You should not restrict your own lifestyle in order to reduce your beneficiaries' tax bill but if you can afford it there are various options and exemptions that could substantially reduce the future liability.

Exemptions

1. There is no inheritance tax between husband and wife.

2. To a U.K charity.

3. Gifts that total £3,000 a year.

4. £250 gifts made to anyone and however many people you like. This cannot be given to the same people as the £3,000.

5. Wedding presents, £5,000 from a parent, £2,500 from a grandparent, £1,000 from friend or family.

6. Part of a divorce settlement.

7. To support female parent-in-law if she is divorced, widowed or separated.

8. Selected agricultural land or business assets and unquoted shares.

Gifts made seven years before death
Any gifts that the deceased made in the last 7 years of his or her life will be liable to inheritance tax on a sliding scale and the value of the gift will also form part of the estate.

In order to reduce the liability you could write any life insurance policies you have under trust and should you die, the benefits of your policies would not form part of your estate, but be payable to your spouse or children, therefore avoiding possible inheritance tax.

Chapter 8

Borrowing money

Every year, according to statistics, we are borrowing more and more money. Indeed, if we look at the papers we can see that we are a 'nation in debt'. However, if you can possibly avoid credit, it is much better to do so. When you buy goods on credit or you borrow money you are, in most cases, taking out a high interest loan. It is the aim of banks to sell money for the highest rate possible in order to make profits. The best bet, at the end of the day, is the consumer. Better than the stock market or any other investment.

Obviously, in some cases you will need to borrow money. The main point is that if you do have to borrow get the best deal possible. Read the small print. It is really surprising how few people shop around for a good deal and end up paying over the odds.

Caution before you borrow

One question that you need to ask yourself before you borrow is: do I really need to borrow? Many people are tempted to borrow money even when they have money saved. This is mainly because it is a nice feeling having money in the bank. However, this is an illusion. The interest you pay on your borrowings will always be more than the savings. To borrow when you have enough in the bank to pay for an item is false economy.

If you do not have savings, you should think very carefully about whether you really need to spend the money now or whether you can wait. If borrowing is absolutely necessary it is important to know what repayments you can afford. The quicker you can clear a loan the less you will pay. Once you have run up credit, make repaying it a priority.

Comparisons of costs

It is a fact that any lender will be happy to give you credit, providing that you are seen as creditworthy. If you are in the process of getting a loan make sure that you have shopped around, including using the Internet. To find the cheapest credit you will need to compare different lenders interest rates in the form of their APR (Annual Percentage Rate). The APR is designed to show the true cost of borrowing, and all lenders must calculate it the same way. Arrangement fees and any other charges must be included in the calculation as well as interests. How and when payments are made is also taken into account. This allows you to make direct comparisons between different forms of borrowing, so check that you are being quoted the APR and not the monthly rate of interest which sounds a lot less but is usually more.

Generally, the lower the APR. the lower the cost of credit, but make sure that the deals that you compare are for the same repayment period. The APR, as the name implies, is the cost of credit over one year at a time. If you spread the repayment of a loan over two years the cost will be more than one year even if the APR is lower.

The APR may not be the only factor to take into account when comparing loans. Some lenders will reduce the APR if you take out protection insurance, usually making the overall package more expensive. You should also consider whether rates are fixed or variable. Fixed rates protect you from rate rises and enable you to budget but your payments won't fall either. If rates are reduced your payments are fixed and will not reduce. This is very much a calculation that you have to make. In today's low interest rate climate it may be that any further reduction may be so negligible as not to affect your judgment.

Payment protection insurance

Payment protection insurance is usually offered with credit nowadays. This again is down to your own judgment. Without a doubt this insurance is useful if you are unemployed or have an accident and cannot pay the loans.

Borrowing to pay off other loans

We are bombarded with moneylenders, or their agents (companies set up to sell money on behalf of others) who tell us how prudent it is to put all your eggs in one basket. This normally involves re-mortgaging. You should try to restrict yourself to conventional lenders. In many cases, it will appear cheaper in the short-term to borrow money over a long period. You will save on the monthly outgoings but pay a lot more over the period of the loan. If you need to go down this route you will probably find that re-mortgaging with a bank or building society will be a lot cheaper than a secured loan.

Overdrafts

If you want to borrow for a short period an authorised overdraft will be a good option, providing that your bank offers competitive terms. Some banks charge arrangement fees for borrowing others will apply relatively high rates. Many will have a combination of both. If you overdraw without permission, which the banks favour, the interest rates charged will double. The advantages of overdrafts are that they are flexible but the amounts that you can borrow are limited.

Credit cards

Credit cards are one of the easiest and most popular ways of borrowing money. They are convenient and flexible and there is no need to approach the lender other than in the first instance when applying for a card. Maximum limits vary depending on your own circumstances, but can be between £1000 and £15000 usually. The balance that you run up on your card can be paid as quickly or slowly as you wish subject to a monthly limit, usually 3% or £5 whichever is the lower.

If you clear your monthly balance in full there will be no interest charge. This means that you can gain up to 59 days interest free credit between the time that the transaction took place and the time that it takes you to pay the bill. If you do not pay the balance in full then interest is charged.

Interest rates on credit cards vary greatly. They can range between 5-20% and more, depending on the deal on offer. Many card companies try to attract customers by offering reduced rates on balance transfers. Some give these low introductory rates on new purchases as well. The introductory rate usually lasts six months. This can be useful if you want to spread the payments over a few months but contain the interest payment.

Buying goods and services by credit card can make sense in other ways. If you use your card to buy something worth between £100 and £30,000 you will normally qualify for extra protection under section 75 of the Consumer Credit Act, which makes the card issuer jointly liable with the supplier if there is a problem with the goods. Other perks can also be offered by the card supplier such as free travel insurance.

Personal loans

Personal loans are offered by many organisations nowadays, with the large supermarkets and insurance companies getting in on the act. These lenders can usually offer competitive rates. So can lenders over the internet. If you want to make a major purchase the vendor will usually offer to arrange a loan but it may be more competitive to seek a personal loan elsewhere.

Personal loans are a useful way of borrowing over the medium term if you cannot get an overdraft to cover the period. Between £5000 and £25000 can normally be obtained over periods of 1-25 years. The more you borrow the lower the APR. You should always carefully scrutinise the rates on offer and don't be misled. If you need a borrowing facility that you can re-use, rather than a one-off sum, some lenders offer flexible loans where you agree a monthly payment and are allowed to borrow a maximum multiple of that amount at any time.

Secured or unsecured loans

Most personal loans are unsecured. This means that if you do not pay the lender can take you to court but does not have the right to seize any property or possessions. With a secured loan assets such as property (usually property) are used, as security and the lender will take a second charge on your property for the value of the loan. This is known as a second charge loan. Nowadays, there is little advantage in taking out a secured loan as you may be able to find a better rate for unsecured loans, unless you have a poor credit rating.

Interest free or low start credit

This type of credit often seems too good to be true. Many people take it up, particularly on cars or furniture. However, nothing is free and you should look carefully at the terms and conditions. You could find that you are signing up to an interest-bearing loan, with interest waived only if you pay up in full during an initial period. If you miss the deadline to pay of the balance then hefty interest charges will be incurred.

The main principle is that you should always check very carefully what it is that you are getting into.

Hire purchase

Hire purchase is still one of the most common forms of car finance. There are several important differences between hire purchase and personal loans: first, unlike a loan which can cover the whole cost, a cash deposit is normally required with hire purchase. This can also be the part exchange value of your car. Secondly, you are effectively hiring the goods rather than acquiring ownership. This means that until the final payment is made the goods do not belong to you. If you fail to make payments the gods will be repossessed.

Credit Unions

Credit unions are becoming an increasingly important low cost way of borrowing money, particularly for people who find conventional borrowing difficult to access. Essentially, credit unions are financial co-operatives set up and run by people with some sort of common bond. Members may work together or belong to the same profession or live on the same estate. The main principle is co-operation.

Members who save regularly are able to get cheap loans. Apart from the low cost you don't need an established credit record to borrow, your savings record and ability to pay will be the main factors when applying for a loan. To find out if there is a credit union you can join, or how to set one up, contact the Association of British Credit Unions.

If you are turned down for credit

Lenders cannot refuse credit on factors such as race, gender or other but they can turn down your application if they think that you may not be able to repay your debt. Lenders usually make a decision as to your credit worthiness by a means of 'credit scoring' and/or by contacting a credit reference agency.

Credit scoring.

Lenders score you on the basis of answers given on your application form. They take into account factors such as whether you own your home or rent, salary, age and occupation. Only those applicants who score above a certain level are deemed credit worthy.

With credit reference agencies, there are a number of specialist organisations which collect factual information about individuals which they pass onto lenders. Their data comes from the electoral roll, other lenders and the courts. This enables potential lenders to find out whether you have defaulted on any other credit agreements, have any County Court Judgments or are bankrupt. Negative information will stay on record for six years. If you are refused credit on the basis of information gained from an agency the lender will give you the name and address of the agency used. You can then contact the agency, with details of yourself and addresses lived in over the last six years and they will supply information. If you find that the information is incorrect then you can ask for it to be corrected and the agency must send the file to any organisation that has asked for it over the last six months.

Chapter 9

Education

With the huge variety of standards in education in different state schools, sometimes parents think that the only option is to educate their children privately at a fee-paying school. Fee-paying schools are used more and more by different socio-economic groups who have built up the fees through a private savings scheme. The number of fee paying schools has grown to a point where nearly 600,000 children are educated there, out of a total of 8.2 million children in receipt of education.

Obviously, fee-paying schools are still going to be the preserve of those who can afford them but this chapter gives an insight into planning for the fees. Fees can vary: at one end of the scale, the cheaper end, it can cost £10,000 per year per child. At the upper end, the Eton's of this world, the fees are much higher. If you are intent on sending your child(ren) to a fee paying school then the only way to do so is to save from the child early age.

If you are fortunate enough to earn enough to save for the Childs education then you will be looking to invest a regular amount or a lump sum into an investment product that will, hopefully, grow at a rate higher than inflation. This could be:

- A savings account or National Savings Certificate (low risk)
- An investment or unit trust (medium to high risk)
- A bond fund (medium to low risk)
- A fixed term annuity (low risk)
- Zero preference shares

Zero preference shares are shares from an investment trust that has split itself into two types of shares. One produces capital growth but zero income. And the other just takes the income. The term 'preference shares means that should the trust go bankrupt these shares get paid before other shares on the creditors list. You would need sound financial advice before purchasing these shares.

Your savings should be invested in as tax efficient a manner as possible, probably ISA or a children's bond. You should also be aware that gifts to a child from someone other than its parents could be tax efficient, as children have their own income tax thresholds so can earn up to that threshold without incurring tax liability.

It is recommended that parents start to invest for their children's school fees as soon as a child arrives as obviously the longer that you save the more money you will have. At pre-school and prep-school, fees are lower than secondary fees and it may be possible for you to pay for them out of income and continue to contribute to a savings scheme.

Many schools offer composition fee schemes, where you start paying to the school before the child gets there. This forward paying entitles you to significant discounts from the school. However, these are only useful if your child attends that particular school. You will not receive interest on the money and will lose out if at the last moment you decide not to send your child to that school.

When advance planning for school fees there are a number of points to consider:

- It can be very disruptive to a Childs education to remove them from a school where they have settled in, so make sure you can afford the fees on an ongoing basis.
- School fees tend to increase faster than the rate of inflation, so make your calculation allowing for an increase of 5% per year.
- You will need to plan for all your children. Make an assumption if you don't know how many you will have.
- Be aware of your own likely income growth.

Bursaries, scholarships and other help

Most independent schools have schemes where help is available to pay fees. They are often small amounts, amounting to several hundred pounds or less. This might make a difference however, if you are having difficulty paying fees. Scholarships are usually for more generous amounts and are awarded to children with talents deemed to be worth developing and supporting. In addition, educational trusts do exist and you might find it useful to make enquiries about these to a local education authority.

If you want more information about investing for school fees and the names of suitable advisors The Independent Schools information service (ISCs) can give you names of suitable firms. They can be found at www.iscis.uk.net and the ISC London and South East Office on 020 7798 1561.

University education

The whole area of university funding has changed in the last 20 years or so and it is now costly to send a child to university. Most parents of children who now go to university received a grant and, other than getting part time work, received their education for free (if they went to university). Now, a contribution to education and maintenance is necessary. The burden of fees and maintenance is now largely met through student loans which only have to be repaid on leaving university. This means that the child will be liable to repay its own loan on leaving university. However, many parents wish to help and again a plan is necessary.

Current costs of university

At current costs it is estimated that £25,800 will be needed over a three-year period, this is without university vacations. This relates to £8600 per year approximately. Some degrees can last considerably longer. The £8600 is comprised of the following:

Rent £3000
Food and essentials £1200
Utilities and insurance £450
Travel £500
Books etc £450
Clothing and cleaning £450
Tuition fees £1,100
Leisure £1400

It must be borne in mind that accommodation off-campus can be more expensive especially in larger cities. In out of control rent environments such as London this needs some careful thought.

Future costs

The government is proposing to introduce a graduate tax (supposedly from 2006 although not yet introduced) where universities will be allowed to 'top up' the current tuition fee of £1100 by up to a further £1900 giving a ceiling of £3000 for tuition fees per student per year. It is expected that the more prestigious universities will charge the full amount. The effects of this top up are that it will, more than likely, add another £6000 of debt to a three-year course.

Student Loan Company

The government has operated its student loan scheme through the Student Loan Company since 1990. For loans taken out by students prior to the academic year 1998, the loans were applied for directly through the SLC and collected by the SLC following graduation, once the graduate was earning over £1752 gross per moth. Now the situation is more complex. Students must apply for support (no longer referred to as a loan) assessments from their local Education Authority (in England and Wales) the Student Award Agency for Scotland (does not apply to domiciled students studying in Scotland there is a different system in place whereby a fixed amount is paid back at the end of the degree)) or the Education and Library Boards in Northern Ireland, depending on residence not proposed university. These bodies make an assessment of the support requirements including parental income. Collection of the support is now done by employers through the Inland Revenue. Payment is at 9% per year once income is over 10% gross. The Student Loans Company still makes the payments and administers loans. Loans are allocated on a year-by-year basis not for the duration of the whole course.

As we have seen above, the outcome of a university education is that students are saddled with debt. Any help that can be given parentally is obviously a bonus. The ways of saving for university fees are the same as saving for other school fees. However, you need to be in a position where you can do this. If you are on the point of sending a child to university then you should make full enquiries to the university of choice about any extra help available if you are on a low income.

Chapter 10

Health Care

Healthcare is one of the most contentious issues in modern day society. It is always in the news and it is used as an ongoing political football. The government tries to provide healthcare 'free at the point of delivery' and to a large extent achieves this aim. However, it is true to say that we are living longer than we used to and we are suffering more diseases and incapacities as a result. This means that the NHS has to treat more people than ever before, and there are greater pressures financially and organizationally.

Private medical care and insurance
In certain cases, it is an advantage to have private medical insurance as you will be able to exercise more choice over where and when you are treated instead of waiting in line with other people to treat what may be a painful condition. The drawback is that private medical care does not come cheap.

It is said that for people under forty, on the whole, private medical care insurance provides poor value for money. It is over the age of forty that insurance starts to provide real benefits. It is estimated that on average people in their twenties and thirties will have in patient treatment once every ten years. The cost of that treatment averages £2000. The costs of premiums over ten years will be in the region of £5000 so the outcome is that you invest more than you get out. Of course, it may be that a serious condition occurs and that you are achieving value for money. However, it is the over-forties who tend to benefit more. Over forty though, premiums start to rise.

If you decide that you want to get private medical insurance there are certain key decisions that you might want to make. If relevant, you should see whether your employer offers such insurance. This is the cheapest option. If, however, this is not an option you will need to shop around for the best deal. Most insurance companies will offer PMI and it is usually through the larger providers of treatment such as BUPA. When selecting which level of cover is appropriate for you, you will be offered a wide range of options. The three standard areas of cover are:

- In-patient treatment (where you stay in hospital overnight or longer)
- Day-patient treatment (where you require supervised recovery time but do not stay overnight
- Out-patient treatment (where you get treatment at a consulting room or surgery)

Generally, most good policies will cover all eventualities but you may have to pay more for out-patient treatment. Other choices you will have to make are:

- Whether you wish unlimited care or a certain amount of cover each year
- Whether you wish to go to any private hospital of your choice or from a selection offered by the insurance company
- Whether cover is only offered is the NHS cannot provide cover within a given period of time (typically 6-12 weeks)
- The size of excess you are willing to pay
- The opportunity to pay for a certain part of the treatment yourself such as consultation)

When applying for PMI you will be required to make a statement about your current health and any previous conditions you may have had. Failure to disclose such conditions can void your policy.

There is a standard list of conditions that insurers tend not to cover. The Association of British Insurers list the following:

- Pre-existing conditions
- GP services
- Long term (chronic illness)
- Accident and emergency admissions
- Drug abuse
- HIV/AIDS
- Infertility
- Normal pregnancy
- Cosmetic surgery
- Gender realignment
- Preventive treatment

- Kidney dialysis
- Mobility aids
- Experimental treatment
- Experimental drugs
- Organ transplant
- War risks
- Injuries arising from dangerous hobbies

Regulatory structure

Almost all PMI providers in the UK are members of the Association of British Insurers (ABI) and registered with the General Insurance Standards Council (GISC). You should check that your provider is registered before signing up to any scheme. If you have any complaint you should take it up with your insurance provider first. If it does not satisfy you, you can then go to the GISC (tell 0845 601 2857) or www.gisc.co.uk. The FSA has taken over general insurance regulation from January 2005.

Long term care

The issue of long-term care is a relatively new one for the finance industry and is little understood by the general public. The structures of the industry and state provision are complex and there are many firms who fail to attain high standards.

Many of us will need long term care in old age. LTC comes in two forms: home care where individuals are looked after in their own homes; and care homes where people go into residential care.

Home care services range from meals on wheels, home alterations to community nursing and day care and respite centres. Local authorities provide the majority of these, but the NHS is responsible for certain areas. The NHS aid is free but usually only available when it is proved that it can improve the patient's medical condition. The general overall rule is that the majority of money is spent on those people most in need.

LTC insurance

These are 'pre-funded' policies where you purchase the cover through payment of regular premiums or with a one-off lump sum payment. You can start the policy at any age, although some insurers only offer policies to people over 40 or 50.

You will decide at the outset as to whether the policy will cover all your LTC expenses or just up to a specified amount and whether it will be a fixed level of insurance or will increase with inflation. Most policies are straightforward insurance only, but you can apply for an investment policy which will pay a capital sum at the end of the term or when you die should you have not used it in all claims. These policies tend to be more expensive.

These are certain risks with LTC insurance:

- The main risk is that you may never need it and if you die before claiming or you stay healthy then the premiums will have been wasted.
- Other risks are that you are purchasing cover for some years in the future (hopefully). It is quite possible that the level of cover may be insufficient for LTC needs. Your insurance company should review the cover every five years.
- The provision of LTC insurance can affect any means tested benefits the state may provide in the future
- Certain illness and disabilities might not be covered. For example mental illness may not be covered.
- Some policies only pay out for a limited time period but most should pay as long as required. This should be checked out when taking out the policy.

The cost of LTCI will depend on age, sex and state of health when taking out the policy.

Immediate needs policies

The downside, as mentioned, of LTCI is that you may never have to claim. Insurance companies will profit out of you. However, this is the risk with most types of insurance. An alternative to funding an ongoing policy is to take out an immediate needs policy.

Immediate needs policies are usually a variant of impaired life annuities. Life annuities are financial policies where in return for your paying a lump sum now, an insurance company guarantees to pay you a regular income each month for the rest of your life. With impaired life annuities insurers tend to be more generous as your life span is considered to be less than it should be.

There are two usual ways to pay for immediate needs policies: with a cash lump sum, or, popularly these days, with equity release. The benefits should be the same as they are determined by the annuity.

These policies are less risky than pre-funded policies as you only purchase one when you know you need it (they are not available until you have a need). However, they are more expensive as the insurance company is almost certain to have to pay you something, although it doesn't know how long. In most cases, when you have purchased an annuity you do not get money back other than the payments. As a result your estate could lose out after your death. Some policies will offer death benefits which are paid out regardless of when the policyholder dies.

Regulators, advisers and providers

From November 2004 the FSA will regulate LTCI provision. This means that all new financial advisors will need to undergo training on LTC issues.

Chapter 11

Stocks and Shares

The investor

Individual investors can be defined as people who, after meeting all their expenses from their income have a surplus left which they wish to invest, one way or another. There are many reasons for investing, the main one being to meet future needs. Investors can keep a cash reserve in a building society or bank, they can invest in something that they think will appreciate in value, such as property, or shares which can be resold when needed.

Purchasing assets

Assets come in many shapes and forms, cash, premium bonds, securities such as shares in a company or gilt-edged stocks (which are government issued bonds), life assurance policies, works of art, property and so on. Each type of asset has different characteristics which will appeal to different investors. The subject of this book is the stock market and therefore we will be discussing stocks and shares as a viable investment.

The first characteristic of an investment that needs to be considered is an annual return: does ownership of a particular commodity entitle the investor to receive any income and if that is the case, what is the level of that income?

Income can be realised in a number of ways. There is the good old fashioned deposit in a bank or building society, which will give a monthly quarterly or annual return but not at rates that will excite the adventurous investor. Gilt-edged bonds pay interest each year, again guaranteed but relatively low. Investment property will produce a rental income and will appreciate in value (in the good times) and the purchase of shares should, in the ideal world, produce a dividend and possibly capital growth, depending on the share. Again, like everything, the more solid the investment, as we shall see, such as in companies characterised as 'Blue Chip' companies, will generally produce stable but lower returns.

An investor will usually consider the return on an asset as an annual percentage of its value. This is the rate of return, or the yield. The rate of return on a share is known as the dividend yield and is calculated in a similar way to interest from a bank or building society: the dividend paid by a company is divided by the price of the share as quoted on the stock market. Dividend payments on shares are not guaranteed. Companies, for a variety of reasons, can decide not to pay a dividend. However, the other rate of return on shares, capital appreciation, is an equally important consideration to an investor.

Capital appreciation is the increase in value of any money invested. If inflation is higher than the rate of return then money will lose value. Shares are similar to other investments in this respect. They can fall in price as well as rise. Essentially, the total return on any asset comprises income received and the increase in value of that asset (capital growth).

Investors will need to look at the possibility of loss on assets. Different assets have different degrees of risk, usually relating to their potential for appreciation or depreciation. Deposits in banks will rarely if ever depreciate as periodic interest will be added and the investment will be protected apart from a possible loss of value due to inflation.

Ordinary shares carry risks of both falling prices and falling returns. A company's declining profits can result in a fall in the share price and also lead to a company deciding not to pay dividends. Many investors will usually try to create a portfolio of shares, ranging from more high-risk equities to safer homes, so that a fall in the value of one is offset by the growth in value of another.

Basically, different assets have different degrees of return. The main principle is that the higher the return the higher the risk.

Investors will also take into account the degree of ease with which they can convert their asset into cash if need arises. This is known as the liquidity of an asset. The liquidity of an asset will affect the return received. The more liquid an asset, as a general principle, the lower the return. Asset liquidity and asset values are also affected by time. For example, the longer that money is tied up in a bank account the more illiquid that it is. Because of uncertainty about the future, money today is worth more than money tomorrow. To bring their values into balance, and to encourage saving and investing rather than spending, the longer that money is unavailable in the present, the greater the reward.

Hedging and speculation

When weighing up which assets to buy or to hold, an investor will keep coming back to the main consideration: risk. The more risk-averse investor will want as much protection of their assets value as possible. There are various means of achieving this. One basic strategy is called hedging, and it is a version of the strategy of portfolio diversification: the investor will hold two or more assets whose risk/return characteristics to some degree offset each other. One typical example is to hold one safe but low return asset for one high-risk one. A more precise way to hedge is to use derivatives, the range of securities whose price depends on or derives from the price of an underlying security. We will be discussing derivatives later in the book. A put-option, for example, gives its owner the right, but not the obligation, to sell a share at a fixed price (the striking price) on or at a certain date. Owning a put option with the share itself means that the investor's potential capital loss is limited to the loss implied should the share fall to the striking price. If it falls further the investor can use the option and sell at the striking price.

The speculator
On the other side of the hedgers trading is the speculator. This is someone who is prepared to take on the extra risk that the hedger wants to avoid. Speculators are in the market with the intention of making as much money as possible. They believe that they know the future prospects for asset prices better than the majority of investors, and hence are prepared to take bigger risks.

Investors, whether hedgers or speculators, who expect a rise in a particular asset price or in the market as a whole are known as bulls, whilst those who express pessimism about the future of the markets are known as bears.

Markets
Assets are bought and sold in markets. Markets are institutions that allow buyers and sellers to trade assets with one another through the discovery of prices with which both are satisfied. Some traders may meet in physical places. However, in the age of technology this is not necessary. Wherever and however the trading is carried out, what is actually happening is a form of auction. For example a trader may have 100 lots of assets to sell. If there are more or less traders at the suggested price (more or less than 100) the trader will lower or raise the price accordingly. This becomes the current market price.

Financial markets can be classified in different ways. One basic distinction is between primary and secondary markets. In primary markets, new money flows from lenders to borrowers as companies and governments seek new funds. In secondary markets investors buy and sell existing assets among themselves. The existence of the secondary market is generally considered to be essential for a good primary market. The more liquid the secondary market, the easier it should be to raise capital in the primary market by persuading investors to take on new assets. The secondary market allows them to sell should they decide that it is an asset that they don't want to hold.

Markets may also be classified by whether or not they are organised, whether they are regulated by an institution. For example, the London Stock Exchange is an organised market while the over-the-counter derivatives market is not.

Markets can be classified by the nature of the assets traded on them: stocks, bonds, derivatives, currencies, commodities and so on. All of these are distinct markets and there are strong connections between them. These connections grow stronger as increasing globalisation and improved technology allows better flows of information. An investor will need this diverse but interlinked information to allow them to compare and contrast different investments.

Chapter 12

Companies

Companies are organisations established for some kind of commerce and with a legal identity separate from their owners. The owners are the shareholders who have the right to part of a company's profit, and who usually have limited liability. This means that their liability is limited to the value of the shares that they own.

Companies are often run by people other than the owners, although in theory it is the ordinary shareholders who control the company. However, the ordinary shareholders will be the last in the queue of claimants should a company go under.

Companies can be classified as limited liability or public limited companies. It is with the latter that we will be concerned here as PLC's as they are known are listed on the stock exchange and their shares are traded on the market, such as the UK Stock Market.

Company data

The primary source for any data and for analysis of a company is its annual report and accounts. These documents will provide all the information on a company's business and financial affairs and its obligations to its shareholders. We will be looking at interpretation of company accounts later in the book.

The annual report and accounts will describe the current trading conditions of the company, what it has sold (its turnover, sales and revenues) and what it has paid out in wages or salaries, rent, raw materials and any other inputs to the costs of production. The documents will also indicate the profit or loss position, the state of assets and liabilities at the start and end of the financial year and the cash flow situation.

Profit and loss

A company's profit and loss account is a statement of the final outcome of all its transactions, all revenues and costs during a given period, usually a year. It shows whether the company made any money in the previous year, how it made the money and how it spends the profits. Comparisons will also be made with previous years and also with other company's performance.

The total value of all goods sold by the company is known as its sales or turnover. Deducting from the turnover the costs of producing goods will give you an operating profit figure. Deducting from that figure, in turn, the costs of interest payments to banks and other parties, will give you a pre-tax profit. It is this profit that is reported in the financial pages.

The next deduction is tax. Corporation tax is paid by the company on profits after all costs have been met except for dividends paid out to ordinary shareholders. Advance corporation tax, which is income tax paid on behalf of ordinary shareholders and their dividend income, is also payable.

Money left once taxation demands have been met is known as after-tax profit or equity earnings. This is now at the disposal of the company for distribution as dividends or reinvestment in the business.

The balance sheet

The balance sheet is a snapshot of a company's capital position at an instant in time and details everything it owns (assets) against everything it owes (liabilities) at year-end. The two sides of a balance sheet, by definition, should balance. Essentially, liabilities are monies borrowed to invest in assets.

A companies assets are made up of two items: fixed or long-term assets, such as building and equipment; current and short term assets, such as stocks of goods for sale, debtors or accounts receivable and cash in the bank. Its liabilities are made up of three items, the first being current or short term liabilities, such as trade credit or accounts payable, tax, dividends and overdrafts at the bank and longer term debt such as loans and mortgages etc.

The third form of liability is that of ordinary funds and this in turn divides into three forms: revenue reserves or retained earnings-the company's trading profits that have not been distributed as dividends; capital reserves-surpluses from sources other than normal trading such as revaluation of fixed assets or gains due to advantageous currency fluctuations; and issued ordinary shares.

Ordinary shares have three different values; their nominal value, the face, or par, value at which they were issued and their book value which is the total of ordinary funds divided by the number of shares in issue; and their market value, the price quoted on the stock exchange.

Cash flow statements

The cash flow statement details the amount of money that flows in and out of a company in a given period of time.

The cash flow statement will track flows of money. The balance sheet is a check of a company's financial health, and the profit and loss account is an indicator of its current success or failure. Together they can be used to calculate a number of valuable ratios. We will be looking at company accounts later.

Companies raising finance

From the perspective of a company, the financial markets exist to raise money through various financial instruments. There are basically three sources of capital: permanent capital of shareholders (also known as equity capital, ordinary shares or in the USA, common stock); ploughed back profits (equity funds or shareholders reserves): various forms of debt or loan capital.

Corporate finance will usually focus on the relative benefits of financing via debt or equity. The relationship between debt and equity is known as gearing (or leverage in the USA), which we will look at later. The more highly geared a company is the more its borrowings compared to its share capital or turnover. A highly geared company will suffer more from interest rate changes and so on. The ratio is calculated as follows:

Total debt liabilities = long-term debt + current or short term liabilities

Balance sheet gearing or
Debt equity ratio (per cent)

$$\frac{\text{Total debt liabilities} \times 100}{\text{Ordinary funds}}$$

Income gearing is an important ratio. This indicates a company's ability to service its debt.

Equity

Equity finance is the capital that allows companies to take the risks inherent in embarking on new business projects. This equity finance is derived from shareholders. There are two common classes of equity capital: ordinary shares, which have no guaranteed amount of dividend payment, but which carry voting rights; and preference shares which usually carry a fixed dividend and have preference over ordinary shareholders if the company is wound-up but carry no voting rights. There are basic variations on these which are discussed throughout the book.

Companies listed on the stock exchange and wishing to raise new equity capital would normally do so by a pre-emption rights issue. This means that existing shareholders have first option on the new shares or the right to sell that option. An increase in the number of ordinary shares in a company without a corresponding increase in its assets or profitability results in a decrease in the value of the shares. This is known as dilution of equity.

To avoid immediate dilution of the shares in issue, a company might use an alternative financial instrument to raise capital, a convertible (also known as a convertible loan stock or a convertible bond). These are debt instruments that can be converted into ordinary or preference shares at a fixed date and price in the future. Their value to a company, besides avoiding dilution, is that in exchange for their potential conversion value, they will carry a lower rate of interest than standard debt.

Company debt

An alternative to share capital as a source of finance is loan capital. This kind of finance is attractive to companies in that it allows the business to be developed without relinquishing ownership and is often more available than equity capital.

Like equity capital, corporate debt takes several different forms. Long-term loans are normally raised by issuing securities; the most common form in the UK is the debenture. Most debentures offer a rate of interest payable ahead of dividends and are often secured on company assets. They usually trade on the stock exchange, involve less risk than equities, but pay a lower rate of interest than other debt.

Other forms of loans include fixed and floating rate note, and deep discount and zero coupon bonds. One of the most recent innovations in debt instruments is the junk bond, a form of finance developed in the USA. This is a bond that offers a higher rate of interest because of the risk entailed. In the 1980's junk bonds were used for the takeover of large companies by relatively smaller ones. They marked an infamous decade with some 'junk bond kings' being imprisoned.

Chapter 13

The Stock Market

Having looked at the general operations of companies which trade on the stock market, we can now turn to the actual stock market itself.

What is a stock market?
Most people know a market as a number of stalls, trading outdoors, from which you can buy almost any commodity. You can buy fruit and vegetables, clothing, travel goods and so on at an outdoor market. There will be the usual smattering of Del boys and Arthur Daly's. A stock market has the same features, buyers and sellers, an agreed price. However in stock markets you will usually also have a middleman, essential to guide the investor through the maze of dealings on offer.

There are many recordings of the first known stock markets in European Cities. In Britain, the first recorded joint stock company was founded in 1553 to finance an expedition to the orient, via a northeast passage. Two of the ships sheltered from storms in Scandinavia and all the crew froze to death. The third reached Archangel and then went overland to Moscow-which was as near to the Orient as they got, and agreed a trading link with The Czar Ivan the Terrible.

There have been many similar ventures. Alongside these ventures London's financial institutions grew. The London Stock Exchange grew out of a small coffee house-the New Jonathans Coffee rooms. As the business grew they moved and eventually in 1801 acquired the name the London Stock Exchange. There used to be a number of stock exchanges dotted around the country but they were eventually amalgamated into one exchange in Old Broad Street London, next to the Bank of England. The stock exchange has since moved as it has had to increase its space as time has moved on and technology and the world markets have grown more complex.

There are two elements to the London Stock Exchange, the first being the official list, which is the main market of the major companies. This is further divided up into groupings by trade. There is a section for distribution, banks, breweries plus one for Techmark (or techMark as it is known) for high-tech companies.

In addition there is the Alternative Investment Market (AIM) (see below) which is for young companies that do not have the trading record demanded for a full listing.

Stock markets now are remote from companies and deal electronically. London's main market operates on a computerised system called the Stock Exchange Electronic Trading System (SETS) for large shares, with a modified version for mid-market companies. SETS is an order matching system that pairs off the instructions sent to the machine by buyers and sellers.

At the moment the smaller shares are using a system called SEAQ, which is based on an American system.

The completed deal is passed to another computer to organize settlement. The Crest system is trying to eliminate the mass of paper by replacing share certificates with an electronic record. Share certificates are still available for those who want them.

Other UK markets-The Alternative Investment Market (AIM)

AIM is usually known by its initials and is a division of the stock market reserved for small businesses. The idea is that the smaller business will grow and mature and graduate to a full listing. The costs of listing on AIM are almost as high as a full listing. However, the hurdles for acceptance on the AIM are lower. There are about 750 companies from a variety of countries listed and the number is growing.

For the smaller investor in Britain there is an added attraction in that Aim listed companies are regarded by the Inland Revenue as unquoted, thus providing access to differing tax relief schemes, including business taper and gift relief for capital gains tax, suitability for the Enterprise Investment Scheme, relief for losses and business property relief for inheritance tax (see section on tax further on in the book).

The downside, and there always is one, is that smaller companies are less secure and more vulnerable to financial problems

TechMark

The London Stock Exchange launched techMark to deal with the business of high tech business, given their importance to the future. The principal aim of this sector is to attract companies involved with new technical ideas - including the Internet – with the promise of rapid growth in their field. As we have seen from recent history, the dot-com boom and bust, this is a risky area for investment and needs a degree of knowledge and also faith in the future of the various ventures.

Ofex

Ofex is one of the growing number of competitors to the main London stock market. Ofex is a derivation of off-exchange. The Ofex system was started in 1995 and trade is done on a computer owned by a stock broking company called J Jenkins. It is a matched-bargain system, so the deal only goes through if there is another willing buyer or seller feeding an order into the computer with a similar view on prices. The fees are fairly low for this type of system.

Virt X

This incorporates a small rival to the London Stock Exchange called Tradepoint, which started as an electronic order book in 1995 and was itself quoted on AIM. In combination with the Swiss Stock Exchange SWX, it created Virt X, with offices in London and Zurich. In addition to trading in the normal UK quoted stocks, it has set up clearance and registry systems to allow trading in Eurotop, the 300 largest companies in Europe.

Shares

Before discussing further the workings of the stock market, it is necessary to have a clear idea of what a 'share' is. When businesses start up, whether large or small, they need money to commence business, expand and then grow. For many businesses, indeed the majority, the initial seed money will come from savings, loans, re-mortgages, friend and family. However, at a later stage of development a company might need to obtain capital from other sources.

Shareholders

A Shareholder is either a person or an institution who, in return for an investment, will purchase shares in a company. The origins of share purchase go back several centuries. A shareholder is not a lender of money but is an owner of the business, or part owner. This means, essentially, that the managers of a company are employed by the shareholders. The shareholders have the right to appoint, and to fire, the board of directors and will, at the end of each year, expect a dividend on their shares, as interest on their investment. Whether or not a dividend is paid depends on the performance of the company.

The stock exchange

In the usual run of events, a company that issues shares will be a 'public company' and will be listed on the stock exchange, which regulates the way that public limited companies do business. The origins of the term 'stock exchange' goes way back into history with no one really knowing where the term came from although there are numerous theories.

Essentially, shares mean part ownership of a company which is the simplest way of understanding the term.

Once a company gets quoted on the stock exchange, there is a continuously updated price for the shares which, usually (hopefully) is far higher than the original share price. There is also a steady stream of people who are willing to buy shares in the company so once an investor puts the shares on the market it is likely that a quick sale can occur, unless the company has obvious problems.

Blue chip shares

Shares have differing status. Obviously, despite reassurances to the contrary, shares can go down as well as up, and investing in the stock market therefore is a gamble. Many people have lost their proverbial shirt 'playing the market'. It is for this reason that lots of investors will turn to the safest companies, those long established companies with a track record of success. These are known as 'Blue Chip' companies. Take a look at the FTSE Index of Shares (the 100 highest performing companies, all blue chip) and you will see that the high performing companies are usually the older companies, such as ICI or the petroleum companies. They have financial muscle, can invest and absorb risk and hire the best managers. The downside of investing in such companies is that the returns are on the lower side, but are stable. The gamble is reduced but returns lower.

Blue chips, like all shares, can never be totally safe. If you look at companies which were on the list a few decades ago many are no longer in existence. So, the gamble, slim though it is, is still there.

Tracker funds

Tracker funds buy most of the shares across the FTSE 100 index so that they avoid being prey to the problems of just a few. In other words, they spread the risk and ensure a steady flow of dividends.

Shareholder benefits

As mentioned, a shareholder will get a dividend on his or her investment. This is a return on the share value. If the company has done well then the value of the share will have increased too so when it is time to sell then there will be an increase in value on their original investment.

Shareholders are also protected in the event of a company going bankrupt in that they can only lose the value of their shares and no more.

It is true to say that longer term shares have proved to be a good investment, trumped only by property which has shown spectacular increases over the last 10 years, with investors receiving a return by way of rental income and also through capital appreciation.

Types of borrowings

Businesses issue a variety of 'paper' which are used to raise capital. In addition to raising capital from shareholders, a company may need to borrow in the short term and longer term and may issue bonds or other forms of paper.

For borrowings a company may issue what is in effect a corporate I.O.U. This will come in the form of a bond. Bonds can be traded, are long term with an undertaking to pay regular interest, at a rate fixed at time of issue (normally) and with a specified date at which they must be redeemed. Some of these bonds are backed by assets of the company and some are unsecured. Like all loans, the interest rate will reflect the status of the bond.

Loan stocks and debentures

Bonds that have no security are called loan stocks or notes. Debentures are underwritten by assets. These types of paper are different from shares in that, notwithstanding the performance of the company they must be repaid at the specified time. Shares, as we have seen, do not.

As the rate of interest on bonds and debentures is fixed the market price of the paper will go up as interest rates go down and vice-versa. This factor underpins the attractiveness or otherwise of bonds as an investment. Because the rate is fixed at issue the investor knows how much the return will be, assuming the company stays solvent, right up to the date of redemption. Any investor in bonds will need to look at the company as a whole and its future prospects of staying afloat before investing.

If an issuer defaults on repayments, usually because of going bankrupt, debenture holders can appoint their own receiver to realise the assets which act as their security and repay them the capital. Unsecured loan stockholders do not have this option but will still rank ahead of shareholders in repayment. There are different types of debentures which will take preference over each other depending on the nature of the paper, i.e. subordinated debentures will have less preference than an unsubordinated debenture.

Warrants

Warrants give the owner the right to buy ordinary shares (equities) usually over a specified period at a predetermined rate, which is known as the strike, or exercise, price. Warrants have a definable value and are traded on the stock market, with the price directly related to the underlying shares. The value is the then market value of the share minus the strike price. For example, if the share currently stands at £2 and the cost of converting the warrant into ordinary shares has been set at £1.50 then the price of the warrant would be 50p. If the shares then increase to £5 then the price of the warrant would be £3.

Preference shares

Preference shares give holders similar rights over a company's shares as ordinary shares. However, usually, holders do not have rights to vote at company meeting. Like bonds they get specified payments at fixed future dates. The name, preference share, signifies their privileged status, since holders of preference shares are entitled to a dividend whether the company is making a profit or not. This obviously will make them attractive to investors who want a fixed income. If the company is not in a position to pay a dividend on a preference share with cumulative entitlements, then the dividend will be 'rolled up' and paid in full when the company is able. Preference shareholders rank higher than ordinary shareholders when it comes to dividends. They rank behind debenture holders and creditors for liquidations and dividends.

There are combinations of various classes of preference shares which will be set out when the shares are purchased.

Convertibles

Certain types of preference shares and corporate bonds are convertible. This basically means that during their lives the holders receive a regular dividend income but there is also a fixed date when the issues can be transformed into ordinary shares. This conversion is at the owner's choice, not the issuers.

Gilts

Gilt is short for gilt-edged securities. These bonds are held to be safe and dependable. They are issued by the British government and, by virtue of being backed by the country as an asset, the risk is seen as zero.

Gilts are issued because politicians mortgage the future of the country. For example, when tax revenues are suffering, because of a dip in the economy, government bonds will be issued. They have a fixed rate of interest and are redeemable at a specified time in the future. There are normally a range of specified dates to ensure more flexibility for the government. The interest rate at issue is determine by the prevailing interest rate and also the target audience, who the specific issue is aimed at. Most gilts on issue are of this type.

There are index-linked gilts and also irredeemable bonds, such as the notorious War Loan, issued to people who backed the national effort during World War Two. Unfortunately, people who backed the war effort ended up with virtually nothing as inflation after the war eroded their value.

The list of gilts being traded along with dates of redemption is extensive. There are shorts (lives of under 5 years), medium dated (between 5-15 years) and longs with over 15 years to redemption. Most quality newspapers carry lists of these bonds and rates of interest. These papers will have the 'yield' rate, one being called the running yield, which is the return you would get at that quoted price and the redemption yield which calculates the stream of interest payments and also the value of holding them to redemption and getting them repaid-always at £100 par, the face value of the security. Since the return on the bonds is fixed at issue, when the price of gilts goes up the yield goes down. Therefore, if you buy a gilt with nominal face value of 100p (£1) and with an interest rate set at issue of 10%, but the current price of that issue is 120p, you would get a yield of 8.3% (10p as a percentage of 120p). If the price of that issue falls to 80p you could get a yield of 12.5% (10p as a percentage of 80p).

There are, in addition to gilts, other public bonds issued by the government at a slightly higher risk. These include bonds issued by local authorities in a bid to raise money, and also overseas governments. The risk is very slight indeed. It is not likely that a local authority would renege on its bonds. Obviously, if you invest in a bond in a country which then undergoes revolution of one sort or another you may be holding worthless paper. It is up to the individual to assess the risk.

There is a very marginal rise in the interest rate of these bonds, because of the perceived slightly higher risk.

Derivatives

Derivatives markets will trade in various things that depend on or derive from, an underlying security inherent in that 'thing'. This security will determine the price of the investment. Basically, there are financial products derived from other financial products. The term 'derivative' is usually taken to cover futures, options and swaps. There are many other complex instruments, some of which are detailed below.

Futures

Futures contracts in the financial markets are generally used by companies and investors in order to protect themselves. The risk will be 'hedged' or offloaded. For example, a business exporting to another country can shield itself against currency fluctuations by buying 'forward' currency. That provides the right to have a currency at a specific rate at a specific date, so that any income from overseas sales can be more accurately predicted.

A futures contract will bind two sides to the agreement to a later transaction, whatever it might be. It is a specific obligation set out to buy or sell an agreed investment or product at an agreed date. For example, an investor decides to buy a futures contract of £10,000 (whatever it might be for). It costs only 10% margin, in this case £1000. Six months later the price has increased to £15,000, so the investor can sell at a £5,000 profit. The opposite can be true with any investment, the price can go down as well as up.

Futures contracts can be sold before the maturity date and the price of the contract will depend on the price of the underlying security.

There is also something called an 'index future' which is an outright bet, similar to backing a horse or other bet, with the money being won or lost depending on the level of index at the time the bet matures. An extension of this is 'spread betting' which most people have heard of but do not understand. The spread betting company. for example will quote a company's shares at 175-200p If you think that the shares will rise by more than that you 'buy' at 175p in units of £10. If you are right and the price goes up to 210p the shares have appreciated by 10p and you have made a profit on your investment. However, if the share price falls then you have made a loss. If the price remains within the same price range then no one wins. Only a small amount of money is paid at the time the contract is made, so the potential profit margin is geared up. This is helped by the absence of capital gains on the proceeds, because it is a bet. This activity, spread betting, is a fast growing activity. However, as with all betting, many people have lost a lot of money and warnings have been issued by the Financial Ombudsman and Financial Services Authority. My own advice would be don't touch spread betting if you have a limited knowledge of the financial markets and of share movements.

Forward contracts

As we have seen, a futures contract is an agreement, about commodities, currencies and financial instruments. Two sides to the contract agree to do a deal at some time in the future. A forward contract is a deal there and then, but for a future delivery. The contract is at a 'spot' price (the price currently prevailing) with a specified date for completion when the goods arrive.

Options

Options provide the right to buy or sell something as opposed to obligations contained within a futures contract. Someone for example, might option film rights for a future date. In relation to shares, buying a 'put' option, as it is known conveys the right to sell a set parcel of shares (usually 1,000) at a specified price at an agreed time. Because the price has been fixed at that time then if the share price has fallen then the investor can make a profit. And, once again, vice versa. The opposite of a 'put' option is a 'call' option where the investor has the right to buy shares at a fixed price in the future. A profit is made if the shares rise substantially in the interim period. If they fall, a loss is made. All that has been lost is the margin of option money.

Options can be traded before maturity. This is known as 'hedging' ones position. For example, if someone knows that they will need funds in a few months time, to fund an aquistion, then if there is a worry that the market may fall in those months, then this is a way of buying protection: buying a put option at roughly today's price.

A basic example is if a company's shares are standing at 65p, it could cost, for example 6p to establish the right to buy shares at that price over the next three months. If the shares go up to 95p in that time then the investor can buy and sell immediately and make a profit of 24p. Like all our other examples there is a downside. If the shares fail to rise above 65p then a loss of 6p has been made.

The situation works the other way as well. If there is a suspicion that a company is about to lose serious value then someone can buy a put option-the right to sell the shares at a specified price- within an agreed set of dates. These rights have a value as well, related to how the share is performing and how long they have to run, so they can be traded, mostly on the London International Futures and Options Exchange (Liffe).

Covered warrants

Covered warrants are fairly recent. They are a more flexible option which is easy to deal with. They originated in Germany in 1989 and are very popular indeed. A covered warrant is the right to sell or buy an asset at a fixed price called the exercise price up to a specified date called the expiry date. This expiry date is anything from three months to five years at issue. The warrant can be based on a whole host of financial instruments or commodities. As with other derivatives investors can use covered warrants to gear up their speculation, as a way of hedging against a market change or for tax planning. Covered warrants are issued by banks or other financial institutions as a pure trading instrument. Covered warrants can be American (exercised at any time before expiry) or European (exercised only on specified date). If a warrant is held to expiry then it is automatically bought back for cash with the issuer paying the difference between the exercise price and the price of the underlying security.

A covered warrant costs less than the underlying security: this provides an element of gearing so when the price of the underlying security moves, the price of the warrant moves further. Warrants are a riskier purchase than the underlying security. A relatively small outlay can produce a large exposure and that makes warrants volatile. They can produce a large return or lose the complete cost of the warrant price, called the premium.

Overseas shares

As with major U.K companies quoted on the stock exchange in London, there are a number of large European and other companies listed. Most of them trade in the U.K so it is possible to get a clear idea of the business patterns and also to invest in them.

The merger of European stock markets has made it relatively easier to gain access to overseas shares. There are a large number of internet based stockbrokers in Germany, France and Holland which make the task easier. You can buy overseas shares through a U.K. based stockbroker, however only a few offer such a service.

If you intend to purchase shares in overseas companies then it is very wise, as with all other share purchases, to carry out some research. There are added levels of risk with overseas shares in that information concerning important variables such as interest rate movements and the economy as a whole, plus the state of particular sectors may not be readily available whereas information concerning the U.K economy is and the overall level of knowledge is greater.

In addition to the above, there is the exchange rate risk. Profits from share trading overseas may be affected by movements in exchange rates.

Chapter 14

Shares and Investments/Unit Trusts

There are benefits connected to the purchase of unit trusts and investment trusts as opposed to individual shares. With trusts you get a spread of investments over a number of companies, cutting the danger of one of the companies going out of business.

Investment trusts

Investment trusts are companies which invest in other companies on behalf of investors. They are termed close-end funds because the number of shares on issue is fixed and does not fluctuate no matter how popular the fund may be. This sort of investment is convenient for small investors who do not have enough money to buy a lot of shares in different companies thereby spreading the risk. An investment trust will have its money spread across a lot of companies so problems with one company will usually be compensated by a boom in another company. Managers of investment trusts are professionals, so, at least in theory, they will do better than the average person. It is true to say that investment companies are as good as their managers so it is wise to pick a company with a good and known track record.

Most investment funds have a lot of money to invest and they will usually invest in blue chip shares, unless specifically set up to invest in a specific type of share.

The cost of the stockbroker is the same as it would be with other dealings and the government stamp duty and the price spread between buying and selling price remains the same.

Although investment trust managers do have a lot of say in the nature and type of investments, investors will also have some say in what goes on by buying the right investment trust shares. There are trusts specializing in the higher risk stock markets such as Budapest, Istanbul and Madrid (called emerging markets); there are some investing in the Pacific Rim and some concentrating in Japan; some go for small companies and some specialize in Europe and the United States and so on. The spread of investments can be very diverse indeed and managers of investment trusts tend to be more adventurous on the whole than managers of unit trusts.

Some trusts are split capital trusts which have a finite life during which one class of share gets all the income, and when it is wound up the other class of share gets the proceeds from selling off the holdings.

Trusts are quoted on the Stock Exchange so the share price can be tracked and also the asset value of the trust can be calculated. The asset value is comprised of the value of the shares that the trust is holding compared with the trusts own share price.

One main reason that many are priced differently than their real value is that major investing institutions avoid trusts. Huge pension funds or insurance companies do not have to buy in to investment expertise as they normally have their own experts. Therefore trusts are used mainly by private investors.

Unit trusts

Unit trusts have the same advantage of spreading risk over a large number of companies and of having the portfolio of shares managed by professionals. However, instead of the units being quoted on the stock market as investment trusts are, investors deal directly with the management company. Therefore the paper issued has no secondary market. The investor cannot sell to anyone other than back to the management company. The market is seen from the manager's viewpoint: it sells units at the offer price and buys them back at the lower 'bid' price, to give it a profit from the spread as well as the management charge. Many unit trust prices are published in quality papers.

These are called 'open-ended' funds, because they are the pooled resources of all investors. If more people want to get into a unit trust it will issue more paper to accommodate them. Unlike the price of investment trust shares, which is set by market demand and can get totally out of line with the market value the price of units is set strictly by the value of shares the trust owns.

Tracker funds

Tracker funds move with the main stock market index-in the U.K that is usually taken to be the FTSE 100. This type of fund is for the less adventurous investor who looks for a virtually risk free return.

Open-ended investment companies

Open Ended Investment companies or OEICs are placed midway between investment trusts and unit trusts. They are incorporated companies and issue shares, like investment companies. Like unit trusts the number of shares on issue depends on how much money investors want to put into the fund. When money is taken out and shares sold back, those shares are cancelled. The companies usually contain a number of shares segmented by specialism. This enables investors to pick the area they prefer and to switch from one fund to another with a minimum of administration and cost.

Advantages of pooled investments

Pooled investments reduce risk and are therefore a safer home for small investors. However, as they are safe they are unlikely to hit the outside chance of a high performer, as individual share speculators might. As stated earlier, there are many different companies and a certain degree of research and knowledge is essential before committing. To be forewarned is to be forearmed. Quality newspapers will have regular league tables of performance. Be careful too with tables that are published showing performance. Obviously, tables can only look backwards to demonstrate past performance and it is the future that matters. Trusts can do very well, but it may be that they have done well in a sector that has expanded and is now contracting.

Management charges for both investment trusts and unit trusts are usually high. One way of avoiding high charges is to opt for a U.S. mutual fund, which is the same as a unit trust and which has lower charges.

There is also the alternative of setting up your own investment vehicle which has become quite popular over the years. Investment clubs, already very popular in the United States are springing up in the U.K. Basically, a group of people together pool cash for investment in the stock market. The usual way is for each member to set aside a regular amount each month and decide where to invest it. This has the advantages of avoiding charges, spreading investments and also the social spin off. Also, the work of researching shares is spread amongst members.

Exchange traded funds

Exchange traded funds are single shares and are traded in the same way but are in effect representative of the whole index, such as the FTSE 100 or the U.S Standard and Poors 500. It is like an investment trust with a holding in every company comprising one of the indices, but there is an unlimited number of shares and the price is directly related to the index. There is a slight deviation from the underlying portfolio price but it is very narrow. That also means they can be used in the same way, including 'selling short' and included in the ISA's. For a small investor it has the comforts of a unit or investment trust plus the reassurance of not outperforming the market. That means you will never do better than an index but will never lose all your money. There is no stamp duty on the dealing because they are Irish registered companies although there is a small management fee charged by the issuers, usually 0.5%.

Chapter 15

Owning Shares

When looking at shares as opposed to other savings investments, it has to be said that the number of ways a person can invest amounts of their hard earned cash is limited.

There are a whole range of savings accounts paying varying rates of interest, ranging from mediocre to high, all dependant on what you want for the future of your savings, i.e. instant access, long term growth and so on.

Property has proved to be a good investment over the years, particularly with the advent of buy-to-let mortgages. An investor can realise an income and also growth in capital value. However, this type of investment is not for everyone, particularly because of the high capital investment at the outset.

Art is another area of investment but again not suitable for everyone as it requires specialist knowledge when purchasing in order to ensure capital growth.

There are a whole range of other collectibles which rely on at least a basic level of knowledge at the outset. Wine is one area and antiques another.

Because most people need access to their capital to fund a whole range of short and longer term projects, such as holidays, education and so on, buying shares usually ranks way down the list as an investment.

Shares are usually a longer-term investment and the risk involved in the investment depends on the timescale of that investment. Rewards can be measured more easily if a longer term has been allowed to elapse.

The stock market provides a fairly good home for investments for those people who are prepared to accept a degree of risk and can wait for the right moment before cashing in and pulling out. Essentially, money invested in the stock market should not be money that you need to realize at short notice or money that will be realized for your old age. The stock market is only for people who have spare cash to invest and can weather the storm if a loss is made. It is not for those who will lay awake at night worrying about losing money on shares.

If you do decide to invest in the stock market, and there are about 12 million people who have done so in the U.K. then don't put everything you have to invest in the market at once. Keep some aside to invest when a really good opportunity arises.

There are two ways to invest in the stock market, long term (suitable for the small investor) and as an active trader.

Long-term investment

It is true to say that in the long term the stock market has produced a better return on investment than any other alternative form of investment. All of the charts produced to indicate growth have demonstrated that over a period of 30, 50 and more years, returns from shares outperform most other investments. Shares in Britain have, since 1918, produced a return of over 12% a year compared with other investments such as government issued gilt edged securities which have produced just over 6%.

This return on shares has been in the face of the periodic cyclical downturns in the economy and in overseas economies. Cash in a deposit account would have produced 5% in the same period. However, cash in a deposit account is safe and as we have seen shares can be a risk.

When considering the long term, questions of future economic stability will always arise. For sure, at different periods economies will fluctuate and losses will occur but in the longer term these tend to even out and share prices rise, as history has demonstrated.

It is up to the investor to decide what they want from an investment. Do you want income or capital growth? These are not absolute alternatives, since companies that do well hand out handsome dividends (usually) and see their share price rise. Unit trusts and investment trusts as we have seen provide good homes for savings and, at the very least will ensure inflationary growth.

Short-term investments

This is another way of investing, but it is for the experts and people who are sufficiently clued up and will devote time to study the markets. This is the short-term active trading which is built on the tactic of taking advantage whenever share prices move sharply enough to make trading beneficial. The active short-term trader will watch the markets very carefully and look for opportunities such as takeovers and mergers where they can buy and sell relatively quickly at a profit.

Short-term investing usually requires more money than longer term investing as the costs of trading can be higher as brokers fees and government taxes have to be paid.

Perks of owning shares

In addition to the usual benefits of owning shares, such as appreciation of capital and dividend income, many companies try to keep shareholders loyal by offering perks, usually in the form of discounts of one form or another. Channel tunnel has travel concessions offered to shareholders, other nationally known companies such as Iceland and Kwik Fit all provide benefits to investors. A number of fund managers will provide a list of companies that provide perks for shareholders.

Chapter 16

Costs of Investment

When considering the initial amount to invest in a parcel of shares, it is important to realise that the less you invest the higher the overall cost of shares, because of fees etc and the more a share has to rise to make a decent return. It is for this reason that most people in an advisory capacity would say that £2,000 is the minimum that should be invested.

For safety the investment should be spread over a number of companies. The old adage 'don't put all of your eggs in one basket' rings very true here. A common portfolio for a small investor should contain at least 12 companies. The main aim of all investing is to get a decent return with the minimum acceptable risk. If you own shares in one company then the risk and possibility of losing your money is greater than if the risk is spread.

It is a general rule that the lower the risk the lower the return. However, the converse holds true, the higher the risk the higher the return. For some people who invest in a single company the rewards can be big if the company does well. In truth what usually happens is that large investments in one company will not produce massive returns or result in loss of all ones investment. The shares will usually carry on rising marginally in the longer term.

Investment clubs

We discussed investment clubs earlier in the book. We saw that they are an alternative to funds managed by professionals and as a result can keep costs down. Investment clubs are a group of private investors who pool their money and decide collectively how it should be invested. There are now over 7,000 investment clubs in the U.K.

The ideal number of people in an investment club is usually between 4-20. If the membership exceeds 20 then the Inland Revenue will term the club a corporation and corporation tax will be payable. There are several stockbrokers, including major banks who have ready-made packages for investment clubs, such as Barclays and Nat West.

There is a specialist charity called pro-share which publishes a handbook on how to start an investment club. The advice contained in this handbook is very useful indeed because, although it is not absolutely necessary to have an in-depth knowledge of the stock market when joining an investment club it is at least useful to know something about the different sectors that you will be investing in.

For investors clubs there are model rules and constitutions that need to be adopted. As with all collective endeavours, from residents associations to enthusiasts clubs, rules and guidelines are essential. Investment club rules will set out, for example, how members can join and leave the club, a unit valuation system that is to be adopted, the decision making process, levels of monthly subscription, meetings, appointment of officers and so on. It is of the utmost importance that procedures are followed as disaster will almost certainly ensue.

It is important to look at whether the club will run indefinitely, accumulating a portfolio or whether it has a specific life, say 5 years.

An investor might be invited to join an existing club so it is important that these rules are already in place and that they are the right ones for you.

A few other tips. Only join in with people that you like and trust. Ensure that their objectives and goals are the same as yours or it could end in tears later down the line. The criteria for choosing investments varies widely from club to club but many will go for the riskier end of the market because the club membership is additional to a members own personal investments. Some investment clubs will go beyond the stock market and invest in property either directly or indirectly through another vehicle.

The main advice given to any club member or would-be member is not to invest in anything that you do not understand. Avoid the overly complex and riskier markets such as derivatives, unless you have an expert on board.

Most clubs invest a small sum, it could be under £80 per month, so this type of investing is just as much fun, and social, as it is serious money making. There are some investment clubs who have had runaway success but, on the whole it is for the smaller investor with other aims in mind.

The cost of dealing in shares

Share dealing can be expensive, particularly in Britain. It is the case that it is more expensive here than in many other countries, and also the whole process is more complex, at least for individual shareholders. True, there have been moves by high street banks and other companies to make the process more transparent but it is still the case that small shareholders find the process rather confusing.

It is also the case that small shareholders are still perceived to be a nuisance, because they deal in small amounts of money which cost just as much to transact as larger deals.

Commission

Commission paid to stockbrokers constitutes the main cost of dealing in shares. Commissions vary depending on the nature of the work and the type of broker. Rates of commission can vary anything from £5 per transaction up to £20 with commission on a sliding scale above the minimum depending on the value of the transaction. An order of £2,000 might cost 1.5% with the rate falling the higher the transaction. There can also be a one-off charge of at least £10 for joining Crest, the UK stock exchanges registry of share holdings.

There are several internet sites, such as www.fool.co.uk which provide information about brokers commissions. It is worth looking at this site before going ahead.

The spread

As well as brokers commission there is the cost of trading. Shares are like other commodities, the costs of buying and selling shares will differ. This difference is known as the 'spread'. Spread varies with risk. Big companies listed on the FTSE 100, such as Barclays, British Airways etc have huge market capitalisations and many shareholders with regular deals every day so would have a narrow spread of say 1-1.5%. A company with few shareholders and little trade would have a spread of up to 10%. The result is that for shareholders of small companies the shares have to rise even higher to realise a profit.

There is lots of free advice concerning shares. However, it is true to say that for the small, first time investor even free advice can be confusing and misleading, given that this advice is often slanted in favour of whoever gives it. It is therefore advisable to use a stockbroker who is seasoned and knows the markets well.

For those with a larger share portfolio it is possible to sub-contract out the management. The stockbroker managing the portfolio will advise on investments but leave the final decision to the investor. The value of portfolios has to be high however, and this will not usually be the route for small investors.

In addition to portfolio management there is discretionary management where a fee is paid to an advisor to provide advice on shares and also the timing of share purchase. The fee paid is quite high, or is based on a percentage and is therefore only useful for those with bigger portfolios.

Income tax

Another consideration to take into account, after everyone has taken their cut, is that of the ever-present Inland Revenue. The government will take its cut by imposing a tax called stamp duty at the rate of .5% on the value of every deal that has used taxed income. The French and German governments do not impose such a tax therefore money can be saved by investing through these exchanges.

Buying shares

The process of buying shares has become markedly easier over the last few decades. In fact, many people have acquired shares through privatisations and through building societies becoming banks, and have not had to use a stockbroker. However, if people want to buy shares in the usual way there are several routes.

The first one is finding a stockbroker. Years ago, this was out of the reach of the small investor. Most stockbrokers operated within exclusive circles. Many did not want to be bothered with the small investor who knew very little, if anything about the markets. Banks have entered the arena with share dealing services and so has a new breed of transaction only brokers (who buy and sell but do not offer advice). However, more and more information is becoming available, through the internet and in newspapers. There has been a trend to present information in a plain English way and the information regarding shares is no different. Finding a broker over the internet is probably the easiest way to get started.

The internet has undermined the closed nature of share dealing and there are a large number of independent companies, most of which are members of The Association Of Private Client Investment Managers and Stockbrokers (see useful addresses). Many have their own web sites.

There are two types of broker: those who give advice and management (if appropriate) and firms who trade only. Phone based and online brokers are of the latter type. People who think that they need help and advice can go to one of the big high street financial institutions with branches round the country. They can also seek out a good local firm that is experienced in the needs of small investors. The best way to find such a firm is by recommendation (like a lot of things) or you can go to the Association of Private Client Investment Managers and Stockbrokers. As mentioned earlier there is the choice of advisory or discretionary services on offer. The latter, discretionary service, is for the larger investor with over £50,000 in their portfolio (although this figure is not fixed and can be lower).

Chapter 17

Internet Broking

Internet broking has, like many other activities on the internet, grown massively. The internet has a lot of real advantages. Investors can place an order whenever they feel ready and can do it from any place any time. In addition, an enormous amount of information is available online to assist with decision making. Dealing on the internet can also be cheaper. It is possible to deal over the net for a flat fee of £10. This is important for those who plan to be active investors and to whom the fees paid are crucial to profit margins. One Paris based research outfit called Blue Sky reckons that the four best value online brokers are all German. Although some online brokers require residence in that country before they will trade, Belgian, Swiss and Luxembourg brokers will trade with anyone regardless of residence.

One acknowledged problem with the web is that it is hard to get a picture of the reliability of the firm that you are dealing with. The web is largely faceless so there are risks of various sorts, such as hacking into your data and so on. Online trading does not generate a share certificate. The shares are still registered to the new owner but it is still computerised and the broker will hold the title to them in a nominee account. This can mean that the investor cannot easily change allegiance to another broker.

To join an online stockbroker, you need to get on to a website and follow instructions for registering. Almost all will require cash deposited with the brokerage. Interest is paid on this money at a low rate. When signing on you register a password which provides secure access for the investor.

If you want to invest in the US you might want to go through a US based broker. These brokers are cheaper than European counterparts.

There is a site that compares the overall performance of several online brokers, this is
www.europeaninvestor.com

There are two sorts of dealing online: one is to e-mail an instruction to a broker who will execute it via his trading screen. In theory he can do that within 15 seconds and within 15 minutes the deal can be confirmed. The other method is called real time dealing in which the investor connects directly to the stock market dealing system.

Normally, when the instruction is given, the broker will 'transact at best'-buy at the lowest available price and sell at the highest. The broker can be set a limit-the maximum at which you are prepared to buy or the minimum price below which you are not prepared to sell. Usually, such limits last for 24 hours although can be longer.

Once the transaction is complete the broker sends a contract note detailing the deal and how much money is to change hands. It may take some time to receive the share certificate but the important element is the presence on the share register.

Chapter 18

Finding out Costs of Shares

The London Stock Exchange has nearly 3,000 companies quoted. There is also the Alternative Investment market (AIM), TechMARK, and Ofex. Most quoted companies are traded infrequently with the most movement taking place within FTSE 100 companies. The FTSE 100 is the main indicator of trends in the stock market. Its name derives from the Financial Times Stock Exchange 100, devised between the FT paper and the actuarial professions. The major companies within the FTSE represent a significant proportion of Britain's industry and exports. There is a large concentration of institutional investment in those companies. The FTSE will change at times to reflect values of companies, which go up and down at times and will always have the top 100 by value. The moment a company drops out of the index its shares will take a fall.

Below the top level in the FTSE 100 there is another tier made up of the next 250 companies measured by market capitalization. Market capitalization means the aggregate value of the issued shares.

All of the above 350 companies are in the lists of the broadsheet papers price pages, which usually contain other companies as well. However, the list cannot be comprehensive such is the volume of the information.

Newspapers will also display a range of other information, including movements in share prices from the close of the previous day. Prices of shares in big companies move continuously and newspapers are often out of kilter with the actual price at any one time. To compound the problem the price printed is the mid-market price, that is the average of the buying and selling price. The internet is one place where accurate up to date information can be found, sometimes for nothing as at www.investment-gateway.com

The spread
Anyone who has bought a second hand car or holiday money will know that the price at which you buy is higher than the price at which you sell. Shares

are the same. The difference between buying and selling-termed 'the spread'-will depend on a range of factors that affect the dealer's risk. One is termed liquidity: how many shares there are available and how many people there are prepared to trade in them. A good measure, as far as the stock market is concerned is how much the price moves when you trade. Massive companies have millions of shares on issue and there is always someone wanting to deal with them. By contrast a small company with a relatively small market capitalization and few shares being traded is difficult to deal with. Therefore, it is easier to buy and sell shares in the bigger companies than in smaller companies. The spread is wider in small, harder-to-trade companies. The width of the spread also depends on the state of the market. In wildly fluctuating shares, market-makers are loath to stick their necks out and carefully widen the spread.

Chapter 19

Interpreting the Markets-Reading the Papers

It is very important to be able to interpret the range of information that is printed in newspapers each day. The frequency and extent of the information will differ slightly depending on the newspaper. The frequency and extent of the information will differ slightly depending on the newspaper. In this chapter we will concentrate on the UK equities market as this is the area which most small investors will be interested in.

As we have seen, an equity is another word for a share or stake in a company. The owner of the share will, hopefully, receive a dividend annually and will enjoy capital appreciation. The equity markets in the UK trade shares across a wide range of companies, from established and stable blue chip companies to the more high-risk ventures.

Although many newspapers do provide information concerning the equities market, and the information is the same, in this chapter we will concentrate on the best known paper dealing with financial information, the financial times, or FT.

The financial times gives in depth daily coverage of the equities market and this consists of the following elements:

- A report daily of the most interesting trading features of the stock market.
- The share price of individual companies.
- Various financial ratios
- Reports on individual companies
- Stock market indices indicating overall progress of equity share prices.

The London share service
The London share service is just about the most comprehensive record of UK market statistics available to the general public and covers around 3,000

shares. The LSS is divided into different industrial classifications. The share service covers companies listed both on the main stock market and also the Alternative Investment market (AIM), discussed earlier.

The standard version of the share service is published in the FT from Tuesday to Saturday in the companies and markets section. The table below indicates the way the information is presented.

Aerospace and defence

1	2	3	4 52 week 5		6	7	8
Notes	Price	Change	High	Low	Yield	P/E	Vol 000's
BAE Systems	229	-2.5	291.5	199.25	3.3	16.8	35.419
Chenning	490.5	-1	491.5	373.5	1.9	13.4	79
Cobham	1367	-32	1460	1237	2.3	14.5	370
Hampson	21.75	-1.5	30	18.25	-78.5	.5	262
Meggitt	297.5	-3.25	300.25	208	2.4	19.0	2756

The symbols below will be indicated alongside shares and can be interpreted as follows:

'A' alongside a share name indicates that it carries no voting rights.

♣ indicates that investors can get a free copy of the company's latest reports and accounts.

♥ this indicates that the stock is not listed in the UK.

♠ this indicates an unregulated collective investment scheme.

Xd means that the recently declared dividend will still be paid to the previous owner of the share.

Xr indicates the same for a rights issue- i.e. the buyer will not be acquiring the right to subscribe to the new issue of shares.

Xc means that the buyer does not get a scrip issue of shares which the company is issuing in lieu of a dividend.

Interpreting the figures

Interpreting the figures is largely self- explanatory.

1. The first column – notes - lists the company name.
2. The second column – price – shows the average (or mid price) of the best buying and selling prices quoted by market makers at the close of market on the previous day, the close being 4.30pm. If trading in the share has been suspended for some reason then this is denoted by a symbol and the price quoted is the price at suspension. The letters 'xfd' following a price mean ex-dividend and indicate that a dividend has been announced but this will not be available to new purchasers.
3. Price change. This will be plus or minus depending on the movement of the shares. This column will give the change in closing price compared with the end of the previous day.
4. Previous price movements. The fourth and fifth columns show the highest and lowest prices recorded for the stock during the past 12 months.
5. Dividend yield. The sixth column shows the percentage return on the share. It is calculated by dividing the dividend by the current share price.
6. Price earning ratio (P/E). The seventh column is the market price of the share divided by the companies earnings (profits) per share in the last 12 month trading period. Yields and P/E ratios move in opposite directions: if the share price rises, since the dividend remains the same, the dividend yield falls; at the same time, since the earnings per share are constant, the P/E ratio rises.
7. The last column, 8, deals with the number of shares traded the previous day rounded to the nearest 1,000.

How to use the information effectively

The first indicator to look at is that of price. The price is the current price of a share. This needs to be looked at in conjunction with the 52 week high and low in order to get some kind of historical perspective of performance of the company.

The prices quoted are the mid-prices between the bid or buying price and the offer or selling price at which marketmakers will trade. The difference between bid and offer is known as the spread and it represents marketmakers profit on any given transaction. The implication of the spread is that investors will only be able to buy at a higher price and sell at a lower price than that quoted in the newspaper.

Volume is an indication of the liquidity of a stock, or how easy it is to buy and sell. High volume is much more preferable than low volume but take into account the fact that smaller companies are traded much less heavily than larger companies. Volumes will also be higher when a company makes an announcement.

The dividend yield is a reflection of the way that the market values a company. If the company is thought to have a high growth rate and is deemed to be a secure business, then its current dividend yield will be low, since the scope for increasing dividends in the future is average.

The dividend, to some degree, is an arbitrary figure, decided at the whim of a company. The figure for the yield is not always a good indicator of the vale of a share. Price/earnings ratios are generally better as they are independent of arbitrary corporate decisions.

Price/earnings ratios are the most commonly used tool of stock market analysis. Essentially, they compare a company's share price with its annual earnings, indicating the number of years that it would take for the company, at its current earning power, to earn an amount equal to its market value. Shares are often described as selling at a number times earnings or on a multiple. In general terms, the higher a company's ratio the more highly rated it is by the market. High price/earnings ratios are usually associated with low yields. A high ratio suggests a growth stock and is, like a low yield, an indicator of an investment where capital growth might be more important than income.

Evaluation of weekly performance
Monday's edition of the financial times will indicate weekly changes in share prices. The column will look as follows:

Weekly tables

1	2	3	4	5	6	7	8
Notes	Price	WK% Change	Div	Div Cov	Mcap £m	Last XD	City line
BAE Systems	♣288.25	4.3	9.5	1.8	9,262	20.4	1890
Chenning	476.5	1.3	9.4	3.9	138.6	11.5	2116

The weekly column indicates:

1. Notes-the name of the company
2. Price with relevant symbol
3. The weeks price change as a percentage
4. Dividend – the dividends paid in the last financial year
5. Dividend cover - the ratio of profits to dividends, calculated by dividing the earnings per share by the dividend per share. This indicates how many times a company's dividend to ordinary shareholders could be paid out of net profits
6. Market capitalisation – this is an indication of the stock market valuation of the company in millions of pounds. It is calculated, as we saw earlier, by multiplying the numbers of shares by their market price.
7. Ex-dividend date – this is the last date on which a share went ex-dividend, expressed as a day and month unless a dividend has not been paid for some time. On and after this date, the rights to the last announced dividend remain with the seller of the stock. The share register is frozen on the xd date and the dividend will be paid to the people on the register at that time. Until it is paid, buyers of the share will not receive the next payment due.
8. Cityline – the FT Cityline code by which real-time shares are available over the telephone by calling 0906 003 or 0906 843 plus the four-digit code for any given share. This telephone information service is designed primarily for investors wanting to keep track of their own investments or the activity of the UK and world stock markets at any point.

The key information from this listing is that of dividend cover. This indicates how safe the dividend is from future cuts. The higher the figure the better able a company will be to maintain its dividends if profits fall.

Other share dealings
Financial times share price coverage is expanded on a weekly basis on ft.com to cover dealings in securities that are not included in the standard share information service. Information is provided on name and stock type plus price.

Trading volume

The back page of the companies and markets section has a useful reference table with the trading volume and basic price information for the constituents of the FTSE Index, the index of the top 100 UK companies. This will deal with the largest capitalised and most actively traded stocks, discussed further on.

Trading volume, price and change in stocks are indicated in this table. Trading volume is an indication of the liquidity of a stock. The higher the figure, the easier it will be to buy or sell significant quantities of stock without having a major impact on its price.

The FT carries three other lists for quick reference on share price movements.

Share rises and falls

This table, shown daily, shows how many securities rose, fell and stayed at the same price level during the previous trading session. It is broken down into nine different categories of security and shows how movements in the main share price indices were reflected in trading across the various market divisions.

Highs and lows

This table shows which shares have, on the previous day reached new high or low points for the past 12 months. The highs and lows table highlights company's that are moving against the general trends of their sector.

Main movers

This table will indicate the stocks that had the biggest percentage rise and falls the previous day. It will indicate the name of the company, the closing price, the days change as a price and percentage.

Winners and losers

Saturday's FT includes a table of the FTSE winners and losers. This lists the top and bottom six performing companies over the previous week in three sectors (the FTSE 100, the FTSE 250 and the FTSE SmallCap sector). Included will be their latest price, percentage price change on the week and change on the start of the year. It also lists the six top and bottom performing industry sectors. There are price tables for unit trusts and gilts. Gilts are normally split into short, medium and long-dated. There are also two undated ones and index-linked stocks. Foreign governments also issue bonds that are listed.

Indices

Newspapers also print information for the movement of specific industrial sectors, plus some describing the type of share. These are then aggregated to form wider industrial indices such as Basic Industries, General Industrials, 650, All Share and so on. The Financial Times produces a full list of the FTSE indices compiled and calculated under formulae developed by actuaries.

Every stock market has its indices to show movements in the market as a whole. Different papers report different selections of these. As mentioned previously, some of the better known ones are the Dow Jones, Nasdaq, Standard and Poor's, Toronto 300. Nikkei, Hang Seng, Dax for Germany, CAC40 for France and the Toronto Composite Index. There is also a table for the highest volumes of trade.

Chapter 20

Shares and Taxation

The area of tax and share dealing has always been a bone of contention.

Dividends

Dividends on shares are usually paid net of tax and the voucher that comes with the payment notification will contain details of a tax credit. People who do not normally pay income tax cannot reclaim the tax already paid on the dividend, and people paying tax at the basic rate need pay no further tax on the income.

People who pay tax at the higher rate have to pay at 32.5% of the gross, though the credit detailed on the slip is set off against this. Essentially, about a quarter of the net dividend is due in tax for higher rate payers.

Scrip issues of shares in lieu of dividend are treated in a similar way. There is no tax to standard rate payers and the higher rates are assumed to have had a 10% tax credit.

If the company buys back shares then the tax situation is the same as a dividend.

Capital profits

A profit on the sale of shares is liable to tax for profits above the basic tax-free allowance. Capital gains tax is only a problem for those people who deal in large amounts of stocks.

Windfall shares received from demutualized building societies or insurance companies are counted as having cost nothing and anything made from their sale is counted as a capital gain, unless they have been put into a tax-sheltering scheme such as an ISA.

There is a tapered tax relief however, so holding a share for a long time will reduce the tax liability. If the shares were bought before April 1998 the price rise can be adjusted for inflation before tax is payable. Dealing costs in buying and selling are allowable against the total gain and there is also an allowance for part paid shares. Gifts between spouses are tax free, so a portfolio can be adjusted to obtain the maximum allowance.

Losses made from selling shares in the same tax year can be set off against the profit. If any of the companies go bankrupt, the shares are seen to have been sold off at that date for nothing and the capital loss from the purchase can also be set off against any gains made.

Share schemes
Receiving shares from an employer counts as pay and is subject to income tax. If the employee buys the shares at a discount to the market price, the employee will pay tax on the discount.

Under approved profit-sharing schemes the company can allocate tax-free shares to workers, although there are many rules attached to this.

Enterprise investment schemes
Investment in newly issued shares of an unlisted company can be set off against income tax at a reduced rate, but the full relief both in income and capital gains taxes comes only if the shares are held for years. Losses can be set off against either capital gains or income. Capital gains can also be deferred by rolling the investment over: after selling the proceeds from one investment it can be invested in another and no tax paid until the investment is realised.

Venture capital trusts
This is a version of Enterprise Investment Schemes. Tax breaks are almost the same but the investment is in a quoted financial vehicle, which will invest the cash in a variety of businesses. The risk is therefore reduced by spreading over a number of ventures.

The above is very brief and for more in depth advice you should refer to an accountant experienced in these matters.

Chapter 21

Pensions

Planning for the future
The main principle with all pension provision is that the sooner you start saving money in a pension plan the more that you will have at retirement. The later that you leave it the less you will have or the more expensive that it will be to create a fund adequate enough for your needs.

In order to gauge your retirement needs, you will need to have a clear idea of your lifestyle, or potential lifestyle in retirement. This is not something that you can plan, or want to plan, at a younger age but the main factor is that the more that you have the easier life will be. There are two main factors which currently underpin retirement:

- Improved health and longevity-we are living longer and we have better health so therefore we are more active
- People are better off-improved state and company pensions

Sources of pension and other retirement income
Government statistics indicate that there is a huge gap between the poorest and richest pensioners in the United Kingdom. No surprise there. The difference between the two groups is about £700 per week. The poorest fifth of pensioners in the UK are reliant mainly on state benefits whilst the wealthier groups have occupational incomes and also personal investment incomes.

When attempting to forecast for future pension needs, there are a number of factors which need to be taken into account:

- Your income needs in retirement and how much of that income you can expect to derive from state pensions
- How much pension that any savings you have will produce

- How long you have to save for
- Projected inflation

1. Income needs in retirement

This is very much a personal decision and will be influenced by a number of factors, such as ongoing housing costs, care costs, projected lifestyle etc. The main factor is that you have enough to live on comfortably. In retirement you will probably take more holidays and want to enjoy your free time. This costs money so your future planning should take into account all your projected needs and costs. The next chapter includes a few calculations about future needs. When calculating future needs, all sources of income should be taken into account.

2. What period to save over

The obvious fact is that, the longer period that you save over the more you will build up and hence the more that you will have in retirement. As time goes on savings are compounded and the value of the pot goes up. One thing is for certain and that is if you leave it too late then you will have to put away a large slice of your income to produce a decent pension. If you plan to retire at an early age then you will need to save more to produce the same benefits. We will discuss saving arrangements further on in this book.

3. Inflation

As prices rise, so your money buys you less. This is the main effect of inflation and to maintain the same level of spending power you will need to save more as time goes on. Many forms of retirement plans will include a calculation for inflation. Currently, inflation is at a reasonable level, 2.75% per annum. However, history shows that the effects of inflation can be corrosive, having risen above 25% per annum in the past. Hopefully, this is now under control

Chapter 22

How Much Income is Needed in Retirement?

Many people need far less in retirement than when actively working. The expenses that exist when working, such as mortgage payments, children and work related expenses do not exist when retired. The average household between 30-49 spends £473 per week and £416 between 50-64. This drops to £263 per week between 65 to 74 and even lower in later retirement (Family Expenditure Survey 2000-1).

However, as might be expected, expenditure on health care increases correspondingly with age. Whilst the state may help with some costs the individual still has to bear a high proportion of expenditure on health related items.

When calculating how much money you will need in retirement, it is useful to use a table in order to list your anticipated expenses as follows:

1. Everyday needs

Item	Annual Total £
Food and other	
Leisure (newspapers etc)	
Pets	
Clothes	
Other household items	
Gardening	
General expenses	

Home expenses

Mortgage/rent	

Service charges/repairs	
Insurance	
Council tax	
Water and other utilities	
Telephone	
TV licence other charges (satellite)	
Other expenses (home help)	

Leisure and general entertainment

Hobbies	
Eating out	
Cinema/theatre	
Holidays	
Other luxuries (smoking/drinking	

Transport

Car expenses	
Car hire	
Petrol etc	
Bus/train fares	

Health

Dental charges	
Optical expenses	
Medical insurance	
Care insurance	
Other health related expenses	

Anniversaries/birthdays etc

Children/grandchildren	
Relatives other than children	
Christmas	

Charitable donations	
Other expenses	

Savings and loans

General savings	
Saving for later retirement	
Other savings	
Loan repayments	

Other

Chapter 23

Sources of Pension

The State pension

The state pension system is based on contributions, the payments made by an individual today funds today's pension payments and for those who are young the future contributions will foot their pension bill. Therefore, the state pension system is not a savings scheme it is a pay-as-you-go system.

Pensions are a major area of government spending and are becoming more and more so. Protecting pensions against inflationary increases have put pressure on respective governments, along with the introduction of a second tier-pension, the state second pension (S2P). This replaced SERPS. The problems of pension provision are set to increase with the numbers of older people outnumbering those in active work, leading to an imbalance in provision. The biggest dilemma facing the government, and future governments, is the problem of convincing people to save for their pensions, therefore taking some of the burden off the state.

Those most at risk in terms of retirement poverty are the lower earners, who quite often do not build up enough contributions to gain a state pension, those who contribute to a state pension but cannot save enough to contribute to a private scheme and disabled people who cannot work or carers who also cannot work. The above is not an exclusive list. The government has recognised the difficulties faced by these groups and have introduced the state second pension and pension credits.

Pension credits

Pension credits began life in October 2003. The credit is designed to top up the resources of pensioners whose income is low. The pension credit has two components: a guarantee credit and a saving credit. The guarantee credit is available to anyone over 60 years of age whose income is less than a set amount called the minimum guarantee. The guarantee will bring income up to £114.05 for a single person and £174.05 for a couple (including same sex couples) (2006-2007). The minimum guarantee is higher for certain categories of disabled people and carers.

The savings credit

Pension credit also has an inbuilt incentive scheme called a savings credit which encourages people to save for their retirement.

The rules are complicated. If a person is aged 65 or over they can claim a credit of 60pence for each £1 of income that they have between two thresholds. The lower threshold is the maximum basic state pension. The upper threshold is the minimum guarantee stated above (£114.05 single and £174.05 couple).This gives a maximum savings threshold of £17.88 single and £23.58 couple (2006-7). Savings credit is reduced by 40p for each £1 of income above the minimum guarantee.

Personal Pension Arrangements

Occupational pensions

We discuss occupational pension schemes in more depth later in this book. Briefly, occupational pension schemes are a very important source of income. They are also one of the best ways to pay into a pension scheme as the employer has to contribute a significant amount to the pot. Over the years the amounts paid into occupational pension schemes has increased significantly. Although there have been a number of incidences of occupational schemes being wound up this is relatively small and they remain a key source of retirement income.

Stakeholder schemes

Stakeholder pension schemes are designed for those people who do not have an employer, or have an employer who does not have an occupational scheme. They therefore cannot pay into an occupational scheme. If an employer does not offer an occupational scheme (many small employers are exempt) they have to arrange access to a stakeholder scheme. Employees do not have to join an occupational scheme offered by employers, instead they can join a stakeholder scheme. Likewise, self-employed people can also join a stakeholder scheme.

Stakeholder schemes have a contribution limit-this being currently £3,600 per year. Anyone who is not earning can also pay into a scheme, up to the limit above. A stakeholder pension is one form of personal pension described below.

The range of personal pensions
Personal pensions are open to anyone, in much the same way as a stakeholder scheme. These are described more fully later on in this book. Employers do not have to offer a personal pension scheme through the workplace, as they do a stakeholder scheme, though a lot do by offering a group scheme which has been separately negotiated with a provider.

Other ways to save for retirement
The government offers certain tax advantages to encourage pension saving. However, the most advantageous savings plan is the Individual Savings Account (ISA) discussed further on in the book.

Chapter 24

The State Pension

Over 96% of single pensioners and 99% of couples receive the basic state pension. Therefore, it is here to stay. Everyone who has paid the appropriate national insurance contributions will be entitled to a state pension. If you are not working you can either receive pension credits, as discussed, or make voluntary contributions.

The basic state pension is paid at a flat rate, currently single person £84.25 per week, married £134.75 (2006-7). A married couple can qualify for a higher pension based on the husband's NI contributions. If the wife has reached pension age her part of the pension is paid directly to her. If the wife is below pension age, the whole pension is paid directly to the husband.

If both members of a couple qualify for a full pension based on their contributions then together they will receive twice the single amount.

Basic state pensions are increased each April in line with price inflation. State pensioners also receive a £10 Christmas bonus and are entitled to winter fuel payments.

At the moment, only married women can claim a pension based on their spouse's NI record. This is set to change and married men who have reached 65 will be able to claim a basic state pension based on their wife's contribution record where the wife reaches state pension age on or after 6th April 2010.

Same sex couples, as a result of the Civil Partnerships Act 2004, have the same rights as heterosexual couples in all aspects of pension provision.

Qualifying for state pension

In order to receive the full basic pension, the main rule is that you will have to have paid NI contributions for at least 90% of the tax years in your working life. If you have only paid for a quarter, for example, you may not get basic state pension. 'Working life' is defined as from the age 16 to retirement age, or the last complete tax year before retirement age. For men and women born after 5th March 1955 the working life is 49 years. For women with a pension age of 60, the working life is 44 years.

If you earn less than what is known as the 'primary threshold' (£97 per week in 2006-7) you do not pay national insurance contributions. However, the year will still count towards building up your basic state pension provided that you earn at least the lower earnings limit (LEL). In 2006-2007 this is £84 per week.

Class 1 contributions

Class 1 contributions are paid if earnings are above the primary threshold. The Threshold, set by government annually, is currently £97 per week (tax year 2006/7). If your earnings are above this set limit then you will be paying contributions at class 1 that build up to a state pension.

The level of contribution is set at 11% of earnings above the primary threshold level up to an upper earnings limit which is £645 in 2006/7. Contributions are paid at 1% of earnings above the upper earnings limit.

If a person earns less than the primary threshold they will not pay NI contributions. The year will still count towards building up a basic state pension provided the earnings are not less than the lower earnings limit. This is £84 at 2006/7.

Class 2 contributions

Self-employed people will build up their NI contributions by paying class 2 contributions. These are paid either by direct debit or by quarterly bill at the rate of £2.10 per week (2006/7).

If profits are below the 'small earnings exception' which is £4465 in 2006/7 then there is a choice of whether or not to pay NI contributions. However, if this option is chosen, then a state pension will not be building up and there could be a loss of other benefits, such as sickness, bereavement and incapacity.

If you are a director of your own company then class 1 contributions will be paid and not class 2.

NI contribution credits

If a person is not working, in some cases they will be credited with NI contributions. This applies in the following circumstances:

- If claiming certain state benefits such as jobseekers allowance, maternity allowance or incapacity benefit
- To men and women under state pension age who have reached 60 but stopped work
- For the years in which a person has had their 16th, 17th or 18th birthday if they were still at school and were born after 5th April 1957.

If a person stays at home in order to look after children or a sick or elderly relative they might qualify for Home Responsibilities Protection. This reduces the number of years of NI contributions that are needed to qualify for a given level of pension. People who are not working and are claiming child benefit will receive Home Responsibilities Protection automatically.

Class 3 contributions

If a person is not paying class 1 or 2 contributions or receiving HRP they can pay class 3 voluntary contributions. These are charged at a flat rate of £7.55 per week (2006/7). They can be paid up to 6 years back to make up any shortfall.

State pensions for people over 80

From the age of 80, all pensioners qualify for an extra 25pence per week If a person does not qualify for a basic state pension or is on a low income then they may be entitled to receive what is called ' an over-80's pension' from the age of 80.

For further advice concerning pensions either go to the government website www.thepensionsservice.gov.uk or refer to the list of useful leaflets at the back of this book.

Additional state pension

S2P replaced the State Earnings Related Pension (SERPS) in April 2002. SERPS was, essentially, a state second tier pension and it was compulsory to pay into this in order to supplement the basic state pension. There were drawbacks however, and many people fell through the net so S2P was introduced to allow other groups to contribute. S2P refined SERPS allowing the following to contribute:

- people caring for children under six and entitled to child benefit
- carers looking after someone who is elderly or disabled, if they are entitled to carers allowance
- certain people who are unable to work because of illness or disability, if they are entitled to long-term incapacity benefit or severe disablement allowance and they have been in the workforce for at least one-tenth of their working life

Self-employed people are excluded from S2P as are employees earning less than the lower earnings limit.

Married women and widows paying class 1 contributions at the reduced rate do not build up additional state pension.

S2P is an earnings related scheme. This means that people on high earnings build up more pension than those on lower earnings. However, people earning at least the lower earnings limit (£645) in 2006/7 but less than the low earnings threshold (£84) in 2006/7 are treated as if they have earnings at that level and so build up more pension than they otherwise would.

Contracting out

A person does not build up state additional pension during periods when they are contracted out. Contracting out means that a person has opted to join an occupational scheme or a personal pensions scheme or stakeholder pension. While contacted out, a person will pay lower National Insurance Contributions on part of earnings or some of the contributions paid by an employee and employer are 'rebated' and paid into the occupational pension scheme or other pension scheme. This is discussed more fully further on in this book.

State graduated pension

The State Graduated pension was an earlier earnings-related pension scheme that ran from 6th April 1961 to 5th April 1975. If a person belonged to this scheme then the national insurance that they paid was related to earnings. The total a person paid was divided into units. For a woman, every £9 paid counts as a unit and for a man every £7.50 counts as a unit. How much graduated pension a person receives depends on the number of units built up. In 2006/7 each unit is worth   a week. In practice, a person might receive less than this if they have been contracted out. Graduated pensions are paid alongside the basic state pension and are increased in line with inflation each year.

Chapter 25

Changes to Private Pension Savings

In 2006, important changes were introduced to the way people save for their pensions. The cumulative changes over the years meant that the whole pension system had become very complex and some streamlining was needed.

The lifetime allowance

From 2006, there is a single lifetime limit on the amount of savings that a person can build up through various pension schemes and plans that are subject to tax relief. The lifetime allowance starts at £1.5 million in the current tax year 2006/7 and will be increased each year. The increases will be aimed at keeping the lifetime limit in line with inflation.

The lifetime allowance applies to savings in all types of pension schemes including occupational pensions and stakeholder schemes. There are, broadly, two types of scheme or plan:

- Defined contribution-with these types of schemes money goes in and is invested with the fund used to buy a pension. Basically, if the fund at retirement is £200,000 then £200,000 lifetime allowance has been used up

- Defined benefit-in this type of scheme, a person is promised a pension of a certain amount usually worked out on the basis of salary before retirement and the length of time that you have been in the scheme. The equation for working out lifetime benefit in this type of scheme is a little more complicated. The pension is first converted into a notional sum (the amount of money it is reckoned is needed to buy a pension of that size). The government sets out a factor that it says will be needed to make the conversion which it has said is 20. If the pension is £20,000 then this is calculated as 20,000 times 20,000 which is £400,000. Therefore £400,000 will be used up from the lifetime allowance.

If a person has already started to take some pension before April 6th 2006, this will be treated as using up a percentage of the lifetime allowance. The pension already started will be multiplied by a factor of 25 to find the amount of lifetime allowance used up. For example, if you are receiving £3,600 per annum this will be multiplied by 25 which means that £90,000 will be deducted from your lifetime allowance for 2006/7.

There are special arrangements to increase the lifetime allowance if at 6th April 2006:

- pension savings already exceed the lifetime allowance. The lifetime allowance is increased in line with the excess. This is called 'primary protection'
- a person is no longer paying into any scheme or plan but has savings built up that they have yet to take as a pension. Provided that a person does not resume actively contributing to any scheme or plan, their savings will be exempt from the lifetime allowance. This is called 'enhanced protection'.

To take advantage of either primary or enhanced protection a person needs to register that intention with the Inland Revenue.

The annual allowance
In addition to the lifetime allowance, there will be a lifetime allowance starting at £215,000 in 2006/7. This is the amount that pension savings may increase each year whether through contributions paid in or to promised benefits. An addition to the promised benefits must be converted to a notional lump sum before it can be compared with the annual allowance. The government has stated that a factor of 10 should be used as a multiplier. For example, if a promised pension increases by £300, this is equivalent to a lump sum of 10 times £300 = £3,000, therefore using up £3000 of the annual allowance. The limit will be revised each year and can be obtained from the government pensions website www.thepensionsservice.gov.uk.

The annual allowance will not start in the year a person starts their pension or die. This gives a person scope to make large last-minute additions to their fund.

If at retirement the value of a pension exceeds the lifetime allowance there will be an income tax charge of 55% on the excess if it is taken as a lump sum, or 25% if it is left in the scheme to be taken as a pension, which is taxable as income.

If the increase in the value of savings in any year exceeds the annual allowance, the excess is taxed at 40%.

Limits to benefits and contributions

The present benefit and contribution limits have been scrapped. The only remaining restrictions are:

- Contributions-the maximum that can be paid in each year is either the amount equal to taxable earnings or £3,600 whichever is the greater
- Tax free lump sum-at retirement a person can take up to one quarter of the value of the total pension fund as a tax free lump sum

In the case of death before retirement, in general savings can be paid out to survivors either as an income or as a lump sum. A lump sum up to the value of the lifetime limit will be tax-free but anything over will be taxed at 55%.

If a person leaves a scheme before two years membership they can take a refund of contributions. Refunds are paid after deduction of tax at 20% on the first £10,800 and 40% on any excess.

Tax relief on contributions will either be given at source or through PAYE if relevant.

Starting a pension

With the exception of ill-health, a person must start their pension at a minimum age, currently 50 but due to rise to 55 by 2010 and maximum age 75. Schemes will administer the rules for retirement in the minimum age to 55. Special rules will safeguard the rights of people in certain occupations to retire earlier provided they had this right already on 10th December 2003, but the lifetime limit will be reduced where it is to be applied at an earlier age. The reduction will be 2.5% of the limit for every year in advance of age 55. Any unused part of the lifetime allowance can be carried forward to set against future pension earnings.

Taking a pension

Savings do not have to be converted into pension in one go. This can be staggered and pension income can be increased as a person winds down from work.

For each tranche of pension started before 75, there is a range of choices. This will depend on the rules of each individual scheme. A person can:

- have a pension paid direct from an occupational pension scheme
- use a pension fund to purchase an annuity to provide a pension for the rest of life
- use part of the pension to buy a limited period annuity lasting just five years leaving the rest invested
- opt for income drawdown which allows taking of a pension whilst leaving the rest invested. The tax-free lump sum could be taken and the rest left invested. The maximum income will be 120% of a standard annuity rate published by the Financial Services Authority. On death the remaining pension fund can be used to provide pensions for dependants or paid to survivors as a lump sum, taxed at 35%.

When a person reaches 75 years of age, they must opt for one of the following choices:

- have a pension paid direct from an occupational scheme
- use the pension fund to buy an annuity to provide a pension for the rest of life or
- opt for an Alternatively Secured Pension or ASP. This is pension draw down but with the maximum income limited to 70% of the annuity rate for a 75 year old. the minimum income is nil. On death, the remaining fund can be used to provide dependants pensions or, if there are no dependants, left to a charity or absorbed into the scheme to help other people's pensions. The person(s) whose pensions are to be enhanced can be nominated by the person whose pension it is.

Chapter 26

Job Related Pensions

The best way to save for retirement is through an occupational pension scheme. Employers will also contribute and pay administration costs. Schemes normally provide an additional package of benefits such as protection if you become disabled, protection for dependants and protection against inflation.

Some pension schemes are related to final salary and provide a pension that equates to a proportion of salary. However, it must be said that a lot of these schemes are winding down.

Tax advantages of occupational schemes

The tax advantages of occupational schemes are:

- a person receives tax relief on the amount that he or she pays into the scheme
- employers contributions count as a tax-free benefit
- capital gains on the contributions build up tax free
- at retirement part of the pension fund can be taken as a tax-free lump sum. The rest is taken as a taxable pension

People aged 65 and over receive more generous tax allowances than younger people. Tax allowances are dealt with further on in the book.

Qualifying to join an occupational scheme

An occupational scheme can be either open to all or restricted to certain groups, i.e. different schemes for different groups. Schemes are not allowed to discriminate in terms of race or gender or any other criteria. Employees do not have to join a scheme and can leave when they wish. There might however be restrictions on rejoining or joining a scheme later on.

Not all employers offer an occupational scheme. Another pension arrangement such as a stakeholder scheme or Group Pension Scheme might be offered.

The amount of pension that a person receives from an occupational scheme will depend in part on the type of scheme that it is. Currently, there are two main types:

- defined benefit schemes, promising a given level of benefit on retirement, usually final salary schemes
- money purchase schemes (defined contribution schemes), where a person builds up their own savings pot. There are hybrid schemes where both the above are on offer but these are not common.

Final salary schemes

With final salary schemes, a person is promised (but not guaranteed) a certain level of pension and other benefits related to earnings. This is independent of what is paid into the scheme. Final salary schemes work well when a person stays with their employer for a long length of time or work in the public sector.

A person in such a scheme will typically pay around 5% of their salary into the scheme with the employer paying the balance of the cost which will be around 10% of salary on average. When the stock market is doing well the employer is safeguarded but when the economic climate is changing, such as at this point in time then the story is somewhat different and the employer has to pay more to maintain the level of pension. This is why such pension schemes are being withdrawn.

The pension received at retirement is based on a formula and related to final salary and years of membership in the scheme. The maximum usually builds up over 40 years. The accrual rate in such a scheme is one sixtieth or one eightieth of salary per year in the scheme.

If a person leaves the pension scheme before retirement they are still entitled to receive a pension from the scheme, based on contributions.

'Final salary' defined

The final salary is defined in the rules of the scheme. It can have a variety of meanings, for example average pay over a number of years, average of the best salary for a number of years out of ten, or earnings on a specified date. What counts are the pensionable earnings, which may mean basic salary, or could include other elements such as overtime, bonus etc.

A lump sum tax-free is included in the scheme which is defined by Inland Revenue rules. The lump sum after 40 years of service will be around 1.5 times the annual salary.

Money purchase schemes

Money purchase pension schemes are like any other forms of savings or investment. Money is paid in and grows in value and the proceeds eventually provide a pension. The scheme is straightforward and has its upsides and downsides. The upside is that it is simple and portable. The downside is that it is related to the growth of the economy and can shrink as well as grow.

It is more difficult to plan for retirement with this kind of scheme, as distinct from the final salary scheme. As we have seen, employers prefer this kind of scheme because, although they pay into it, it doesn't place any onerous responsibilities on them.

The pension that is received on retirement will depend on the amount paid into the scheme, charges deducted for management of the scheme, how well the investment grows and the rate, called the annuity rate, at which the fund can be converted into pension. A major problem for pension schemes has been the decline in annuity rates in recent years.

With most money purchase schemes the proceeds are usually given to an insurer who will administer the funds. The trustees of the scheme will choose the insurer, in most cases. In some cases, contributors are given the choice of investment. This choice will usually include:

- a with-profits basis which is a medium-risk option and which is safer and more likely to provide a good return if a person remains with the same employer. The value of the fund cannot fall and will grow steadily as reversionary bonuses are added. On retirement a person will receive a terminal bonus, which represents a chunk of the overall return
- a unit linked fund- where money is invested in one or more funds, e.g. shares, property, gilts and so on.

The cash balance scheme

A cash balance scheme lies somewhere between a final salary scheme and a money purchase scheme. Whereas in a final salary scheme a person is promised a certain level of pension at retirement with a cash balance scheme a person is promised a certain amount of money with which to buy a pension. The amount of cash can be expressed in a number of ways, for example as a percentage of salary per annum for each year of membership. So if a person is earning £50,000 per annum and the cash balance scheme is promising 15% of salary for each year of membership, there would be a pension fund of £50,000 times 15% which equals £75,000 after 10 years of membership.

Tax

Whichever type of pension that is offered, the government sets limits on maximum amounts that a person can receive. The Inland Revenue sets limits on occupational schemes which relate mainly to final salary schemes and which are shown below.

Main Inland Revenue limits on pensions.

1. If you are in a scheme set up on or after 14th March 1989 or a scheme set up before 14th March 1989 but you joined on or after 1st June 1989, or are in a scheme set up before 14th March 1989 which you joined on or after 17th March 1987 but before 1st June 1989 if you elected to be treated under the 'post 1989 regime'.

Under the above rules you will get a percentage of final salary up to £68,000 with a limit on the lump sum at retirement of 1.5 times final salary up to a maximum of £150,000. These are the limits for the current tax year.

2. If you are in a scheme set up before 14th March 1989 which was joined on or after 17th March 1987 and before 1st June 1989 you will receive a percentage of final salary up to a maximum of 1.5 times salary or £150,000.

If you joined a scheme before 17th March 1987 you will receive a percentage of final salary up to 1.5 times salary.

Normally, the maximum pension and any other benefits build up over a long period, usually 40 years. The pension builds up at a rate of one sixtieth of final salary for each year that you are with the employer. The maximum lump sum builds up at a rate of three-eightieths of final salary.

The rules allow for a faster build up of pension if a person can't build up pension over such a long period.

The pension scheme will set a pension age, and although there used to be difference in the age at which pension was paid to men and women respectively, the dates are now usually harmonised. The most popular age for receiving pension is 65 although some opt for 60. The lowest age at which pensions can be paid is 50. In most cases, a person must give up a job before receiving an occupational pension from an employer. The rules are in the process of changing so that a pension can be received from an employer whilst still working for that employer.

Tax rules set a limit on the amount that a pension can be increased each year. This is usually inflation. If the starting pension is less than the Inland Revenue maximum then bigger increases are allowed. For pensions built up from April 6th 1997 onwards the increase is limited to a limited price indexation which means that each year the pension can be increased in line with inflation up to a maximum of 2.5% per year.

Contributions into occupational schemes

Some occupational schemes are non-contributory, which means that the employer pays all contributions. The majority of schemes, however, are contributory, with the employer and employee contributing. Usually, the employee will pay 5% of salary. With money purchase schemes the employer will also pay a specified amount of salary. With final salary schemes, which as stated are becoming less and less common, the employer will make up the balance needed to provide the specified amount.

Both employer and employee will get tax relief on contributions.

The Inland Revenue will limit the amount that a person can contribute to an occupational pension scheme. The limit is currently 15% of earnings. There is an upper limit on the amount that can qualify for tax relief. Check the current limit with the Inland Revenue.

There is no Inland Revenue limit to what an employer can put into a scheme although there are rules to prevent paying in more than is needed to provide the maximum possible benefits.

Top-up schemes exist which can be used to top up pension pots but these are liable for tax in the usual way. There are two main types of top-up scheme:

- Unfunded schemes. With these schemes, an employer simply pays benefits at the time that a person reaches retirement. Income tax will be due on any benefits, even on lump sums
- funded schemes (Funded Unapproved Retirement Benefit Schemes or FURBS). This is where the employer pays contributions which build up funds to provide the eventual benefits. At the time that contributions are made they count as tax-liable fringe benefits. Usually the fund is arranged as a trust, which attracts only normal rates of tax. The benefits are tax-free when they are paid out, having been subject to tax.

If an employer runs a scheme which a person is eligible to join they must be given information about it automatically. The rules are as follows:

- an explanatory booklet must be given within two months of commencing employment if eligible to join, or within 13 weeks of joining
- each year a summary trustees report an annual accounts must be given
- employees can request a copy of the full accounts which must be provided on request
- an annual benefit statement must be provided
- options on leaving the scheme and benefit entitlements, transfer value must be provided within 3 months of request
- any announcements of changes to the scheme must be given to the scheme member within one month of the change being made

Information about employer schemes can be found in various booklets listed in the appendix to this book.

Chapter 27

Group Personal Pension Schemes

Group personal pension schemes are a popular alternative to occupational pension schemes, particularly to smaller employers.

Group personal pension schemes are not occupational pension schemes. They are pension schemes tailored to employees of a company. The employer is not obliged to pay anything into such schemes, although many do. The amount an employer will pay is often less than an occupational pension scheme. The employee will usually end up contributing more.

Group personal pension schemes work on a money purchase basis, and, as we have seen, the employee will bear all the risks themselves. The administration charges for group personal pension schemes are usually the same as other pension funds.

A plus side of group schemes is that they are seen to be particularly suitable for employees on short term contracts who cannot build up reasonable benefits in an occupational scheme because of frequent job changes. Group pension schemes are personal and travel with the employee and can be kept going without a break.

Group Personal pension Schemes and stakeholder schemes

Since October 2001, employers with more than five employees must offer at least an occupational pension scheme, a group scheme or a stakeholder scheme to employees. Stakeholder schemes are outlined further on in the book.

The pension on retirement from a group scheme will depend on the same factors as all money purchase schemes, such as the overall amount paid in and the performance of the investment. In addition, the charges taken to administer the scheme will influence the amount left in the pot.

In terms of receipt of a tax-free lump sum, group schemes are exactly the same as all other pension funds.

Chapter 28

Contracting Out Through Occupational Schemes

Employees who are building up a state additional pension can contract out, which means that a person gives up their additional state pension and instead builds up a replacement through an occupational scheme or a personal pension scheme.

Contracting out essentially means that a person receives less pension at retirement from the state. Because this saves the state money then it pays back part of the NI contributions that the employee and employer are paying now. These repayments are invested in the personal or occupational scheme to raise its value.

Contracting out has not benefited everyone and how much it benefits an individual depends on how much is given up on the value of the additional state pension. This in turn depends very much on the type of scheme that is used to contract out.

Although in many cases, an individual has the choice whether or not to contract out, if an employee belongs to a contracted out fund then the choice has already been made. The only way to rejoin S2P would be to leave the scheme.

How contracting out operates in an occupational scheme

As stated, if a person is contracted out in an occupational pension scheme, then both employee and employer will pay lower NI contributions which are reinvested in the scheme.

Contracting out before 6th April 1997

During the period between 6th April 1978 and 6th April 1997, contracting out meant giving up the State Earnings Related Pension (SERPS). For pension rights built up over the period up to 6th April 1997, the occupational scheme guarantees to pay a minimum amount of pension at retirement, known as a

Guaranteed Minimum Pension (GMP). It will also pay a guaranteed widow's or widowers pension. This Guaranteed Pension will be broadly equivalent to the amount that would have been built up in SERPS.

Contracted out final salary pension rights are different for pensions built up from 6th April 1997. A person no longer builds up any Guaranteed Pension Rights. Instead the employer must run a scheme which, for nine out of ten scheme members, is at least as good as a reference scheme which has been specified by the government. The main elements of such a reference scheme are that it must provide:

- a retirement pension at age 65 equal to one eightieth of qualifying earnings for each year of membership since April 1997, up to a maximum pension of half average earnings. Earnings to be used in the calculation are 90% of total earnings, including overtime and bonuses etc, above the lower earnings limit up to the upper limit. Earnings for the last three years before retirement or leaving the scheme are averaged. The pension must be the same for both men and women and can be paid before 65 but will be reduced.
- A widows or widowers pension equal to half the retirement pension built up if the scheme member dies either while working, after retirement or having moved on to another job while leaving the pension behind in the previous employers scheme
- Annual increases to pensions, once they start to be paid, of inflation up to 5% maximum.

Each scheme has to have a certificate from an actuary stating that its benefits are sufficient to pass the contracting out test.

Rules for contracting out from 6th April 2002

From 6th April 2002, a person contracts out of S2P instead of SERPS. As discussed, pensions provided by S2P for people on low to moderate incomes are higher than SERPS. To ensure that people still had an incentive to contract out of S2P certain rules were introduced. People earning less than the Band 3 threshold will continue to build up some residual S2P pension even though are contracted out. This means that at retirement they will get some enhanced pension through S2P.

For people earning between the lower earnings limit and the low earning threshold, currently £84 and £97 (2006/7) their residual SERPS pension will be based on the difference between their actual earnings and the low earnings threshold. For people earning more than the low earnings threshold up to the Band 3 threshold their residual S2P will be based on the difference between the SERPS pension they would have had if SERPS had not been abolished and the S2P they would have had if they had not contracted out.

There are no special rules for people above the Band 3 threshold, because for them S2P is the same as SERPS pension they would have got had SERPS not been abolished.

Contracting out through an occupational money purchase scheme
Contracting out through an occupational money purchase scheme is different. Employer and employee still both pay lower NI contributions. However, the employer scheme makes no guarantee about how much it will pay to replace the state pension. Instead the employer is required to guarantee that they will pay a set amount into the scheme that will build up the fund. The amounts invested are equal to the amounts that the employer and the employee have saved by paying lower NI contributions. The fund that is built up provides a set of benefits called 'protected rights' which comprise:

- a retirement pension which can be paid from age 60 onwards
- a pension for widow or widower if a person dies before retirement
- a pension for widow or widower if death happens if death occurs after retirement which is equal to half the pension that is received. A person can opt for a larger pension for their self with no provision for widow or widower
- increases to pensions once they start to be paid. Although this requirement may be removed.

After April 2006 up to a quarter of the pension savings can be taken as a tax-free lump sum.

Protected rights benefits build up on a money purchase basis so the amount of money that you receive as a pension will depend on:

- the amount invested

- Charges deducted from the scheme
- How well the investment does
- The rate (annuity rate) at which the pension fund can be converted into a pension.

Contracting out before 6th April 1997 and after 6th April 1997

Up to 6th April 1997 the amount of National Insurance rebate which an employer was obliged to invest for protected rights was a flat rate, the same for everyone. Where a person has built up protected rights before 6th April 1997, the DWP will work out the full SERPS pension that a person would have built up had they not contracted out. The amount built up is called the 'notional GMP' and it may be more or less than the protected rights pension that is received from the contracted out scheme. Whatever is left after subtracting the notional GMP is the amount of SERPS pension that will be received from the state.

From 1997 onwards, the rules for rebates changed. They are now age related. The older a person is the larger the rebate.

Personal pension plans

If an employer's pension scheme is not contracted out of the state scheme a person can opt to contract out on his or her own through a special personal pension called a ' rebate-only plan. If a person belongs to a group personal pension scheme offered by an employer they will have their own personal pension plan.

Free-standing Additional Voluntary Contributions

If a person belongs to an employer scheme that is not contracted out they can contract out independently using a free-standing additional voluntary contribution scheme instead of a personal pension. However, it is usually better to take out a personal pension plan as overall the benefits are better. The DWP pays less into a contracted out AVC scheme than it does into a contracted out personal pension.

Other benefits from occupational schemes

Occupational pensions schemes, as opposed to group personal or stakeholder pension schemes, automatically provide packages of benefits. These will include:

- lump-sum life cover and dependants pensions if death occurs before retirement
- dependants pensions if death occurs after retirement
- replacement income if a person has to give up work early because of ill-health or disability
- a pension if retirement occurs before normal retirement age

The Inland Revenue sets limits on the amounts that dependants can receive by way of pension after death.

Like the retirement pension itself, the benefits are subsidised because the employer pays some or all of the costs of provision, and a person will get tax relief on the contributions.

A widows or widower's pension is usually paid automatically to wife or husband. partner or civil partner. Most occupational schemes usually allow the pension to be paid to someone else at the trustee's discretion. If the trustee's decide that there is no eligible person to receive it then the money remains in the scheme.

Pensions can be paid to other dependants, such as children in addition to any amount paid to a widow, widower or partner. Any one pension cannot be more than two-thirds of the maximum retirement pension that the person would have received if he or she had been alive. A pension for a dependant child ceases when that child ceases to be dependant, for example when the child reaches the age of 18, or when he or she finishes full-time education. Pensions for other dependants can continue for the rest of their lives even if they cease to be dependant.

Early retirement due to ill-health
There are no Inland Revenue limits on the age that a person can receive a pension if they have to retire through ill-health. A person does not have to be completely incapable of work to qualify for the pension. If health is sufficiently bad to prevent a person from pursuing a normal course of work then this will qualify. However, evidence of ill-health will be needed and each scheme will set its own rules. Tax limits on the pension that is received are more generous than those that apply to retirement for other reasons. The pensions and benefits that are received cannot be more than the pension that would be received had a person worked until normal retirement age.

If a person is severely ill and not expected to live long then the pension can be converted into a lump sum. There is a tax charge of 20% on the part that could not be taken as a tax-free lump sum.

Early retirement

For pension schemes set up before 14th March 1989, tax rules will normally prohibit an employer pension scheme from paying a full pension before the normal retirement age for the scheme. For these schemes, the earliest retirement age allowed by the Inland Revenue is either 55 or 60, depending on when the scheme was set up and when it was joined. In practice, most schemes set their own early retirement age later than this. The most common retirement age is 65, the second most common is 60.

Under the tax rules for most pre-March 1989 schemes, the earliest age at which any retirement pension can be paid is 50 for men and 45 for women (provided that the women is within 10 years of the normal retirement age). This is due to be increased to 55 from 2010.

A person can start to receive a pension from a protected rights scheme from age 60.

Chapter 29

Leaving an Occupational Scheme

There are a number of reasons why people may want to leave an occupational scheme before retirement. One of the main ones is leaving an employer to take up another job. It could be that there is a desire to leave one pension scheme and enter another. Whatever the reason, there are a number of questions that need answering.

If a person leaves an occupational pension fund and has been a member of it for two years or more that scheme must provide a pension at retirement, called a deferred pension, or allow transfer of the contributions. A new pension scheme is not legally obliged to accept transfer.

Obtaining a refund of contributions

If a person leaves a scheme that he or she has belonged to for less than two years, there is no automatic entitlement to a refund or pension. A person can have back any contributions that they themselves paid but not their employer. Tax is paid on any refund. There may also be a deduction. A significant reduction, if a person had been contracted out of SERPS prior to April 1997 through the occupational scheme. The scheme may arrange for a person to be 'bought back into' the state scheme for the period that has been contracted out. This will cost a sum of money, called the Contribution Equivalent Premium, to the state.

For periods of contracting out after April 1997, it is no longer possible for a person to be bought back into SERPS, if membership of the scheme has been less than two years.

If a person has contracted out through a final-salary scheme and leaves, the scheme is obliged to protect contracted out pension rights. For contracted out pension rights built up before April 1997, a person is entitled to a Preserved Guaranteed Minimum Pension (GMP) and widows or widower's pension. The amount of GMP is calculated and increased from the date that a person leaves a pension. The increase can either be in line with inflation, in line with average earnings, or by a fixed amount. GMP's can be transferred to another scheme or plan as long as that scheme or plan can be used for contracted out pension rights.

For periods of contracting out after 6th April 1997, a person can no longer build up GMPs. Instead the scheme has to provide a person with a scheme of benefits that is at least as good as those from a reference scheme. If a person leaves the scheme and leaves the benefits there then they must be increased by inflation up to a maximum each year. f a person leaves a contracted out money purchase scheme that scheme must continue to provide protected rights. tories of people losing touch with their pensions over the years are legion and it is very important to stay in touch with the scheme and inform them of change of address and change of circumstances. There is the right to request a statement of benefits once every twelve months.

Chapter 30

Transferring Pension Rights

Since 1st January 1986 anyone leaving an employer pension scheme who has a right to a preserved pension also has the right to take a transfer value instead. This is a lump sum that is judged to be equivalent to the preserved pension and any other rights given up. This cannot be received in the hand but can be transferred.

If pension rights are switched from an occupational money purchase scheme, the transfer value will quite simply be the value of that fund. If the switch is from a final salary scheme the transfer value must be worked out by an actuary. Assumptions are made about future investment growth and a lump sum to be transferred is arrived at.

If a person transfers into a money purchase scheme the sum is simply added to the fund. If it is transferred into a final salary scheme the transfer might be used to buy a fixed amount of pension at retirement, buy extra years in a fund or invested as a separate fund to be used at retirement to buy 'extra benefits' in a scheme. The pension fund that is the recipient of the fund will provide advice in this area.

Transfer to a Section 32 plan

Section 32 plans – termed buy-back bonds – are a special type of personal pension designed to accept transfer value from occupational pension schemes. The transfer value is simply transferred into the plan and used to buy a deferred annuity, which is an insurance product designed to pay out an income starting at a future date.

The decision whether to transfer from a previous employers occupational scheme has never been an easy one and many people feel that they will suffer a shortfall if they do. The benefits of transfer need to be weighed up on the basis of what information can be gathered from the new provider.

Public sector transfers can be easier as 'transfer clubs' exist. This is related to final salary schemes and allows the transfer years that have been built up to be added to the new schemes.

It is the transfer from an employer's occupational scheme to a personal pension scheme that can be problematic and where losses can occur. If the old scheme is a final salary scheme there will inevitably be loss of benefits associated with the old scheme, benefits such as transferring pension to dependants if death occurs. With occupational schemes quite often the employer will bear the cost of administration expenses whereas this will not be the case with a personal pension scheme.

Therefore, a lot of thought needs to be given to transferring into a personal pensions scheme, and as much information as possible gathered before doing so.

Winding up of occupational pension schemes

If an occupational scheme is wound up by an employer, for whatever reason, for example bankruptcy or being taken over by another firm which doesn't wish to continue the scheme, the pension entitlement from the scheme will depend on the rules of the particular scheme. Whilst some are generous others may provide only the minimum entitlement.

There are rules which make any shortfall in final salary schemes a debt of the company. Where bankruptcy occurs the debt will rank alongside that of other unsecured creditors. This is not a good position to be in as it invariably means that pensions become non-existent, although since September 2003, the position of unsecured creditors in relation to pension rights became a little stronger. There is a pecking order, as there always is in bankruptcy and the rights of those with pension funds can be obtained from the government insolvency service website. See also useful addresses at the back of this book.

Chapter 31

Pension Schemes and Regulation

Pension schemes must either be a statutory scheme or be run at arms length from an employer and their business. The Robert Maxwell debacle that happened in 1991, was a wake up call to the pensions industry. Pensioners in the Mirror Group Newspapers scheme lost £440 million pounds, looted by Maxwell. As well as being the owner of the company he was a trustee of the pension scheme and had unprecedented access to the money in the fund.

Statutory schemes are set up through Acts of Parliament and is the usual arrangement for most public sector workers. Non-statutory schemes are usually set up as trusts and are regulated by laws which are applicable to them. Assets are given to trustees to manage and the trustees are responsible for investing the money in such a way as to ensure that the long-term aims of the trust are achieved, that is to provide adequate pensions to contributors to a scheme.

The pensions regulator

The Occupational Pensions Regulatory Authority is responsible for overseeing occupational schemes. Moves are afoot to replace OPRA with a body with more powers to regulate.

Pension Trustees

Anyone can become a pension fund trustee. The employer will be represented and other professional individuals will usually sit on the board of trustees of pension funds. There is the requirement that at least a third of the trustees will be nominated by members.

Trustees obviously have a very important role in the administration of pension schemes. They are required to have appropriate knowledge and understanding of the scheme and the laws surrounding it.

Virtually all pension schemes through the trustees will use advisors, as a matter of necessity. Advisors will take the shape and form of financial and legal advisors. It is they who will provide the specialist knowledge need to be able to administer the pension fund effective.

Chapter 32

Options For Those Who Cannot Access an Occupational Scheme

If a person is self-employed, with an employer who does not run an occupational scheme, or eligible to join an occupational scheme, belongs to a group personal pension scheme, a stakeholder scheme or simply have not joined a scheme, for example run their own business and haven't got round to it, there are a number of options to consider.

For people who are self employed, or in any of the situations mentioned above, it is quite often the case that it is difficult enough balancing the personal books without having to consider putting a monthly amount aside for a pension. However, it is crucial that this is done as time goes by and it is important to ensure that a pension is provided at the end of the working life.

The longer that pension contributions are delayed the more expensive that it become to make adequate provision.

The table below shows the amount that an individual needs to save and at what age to provide each £10,000 a year of pension by the age of 65. Please bear in mind that these figures change and any pension provider can provide up to date figures.

Age at which start regular   Monthly amount required
Contributions

Age at which start regular Contributions	Monthly amount required
20	£190
30	£282
40	£456
50	£877
60	£3,037

Contributions will increase each year in line with earnings.

Chapter 33

Options for savings

Personal pensions

We have discussed personal pensions as an option of saving for retirement. Savings are usually with an insurance company, through unit trusts. Banks and building societies can also offer these pension plans.

All personal pension plans operate on a money-purchase basis, basically the fund grows over time and provides a pension to the contributor. The drawback with money purchase schemes is that they offer no guarantees at all and depend very much on the performance of the stock market or other sectors of the economy. Therefore the pension at the end cannot be guaranteed. Another important factor is the annuity rate at the time of retirement (the amount of pension that the fund can buy).

Qualifications for a personal pension

Nearly everyone under the age of 75 can qualify for a personal pension. The only people who cannot have a personal pension scheme are controlling directors who already belong to an occupational scheme and employees earning more than £30,000 a year who already belong to an occupational scheme.

With personal pension schemes, as with occupational schemes, a person can usually take a tax-free lump sum on retirement. This will reduce the amount of pension that a person gets. The amount of the lump sum will depend on the rules of the scheme.

A person doesn't have to stop work in order to take a pension from a personal plan. There are, as mentioned throughout this book, rules governing age that a person can take the pension. Usually, a person can start from 50 years of age upwards. People over 75 are prohibited from paying into a personal pension plan.

What amounts to pay into a personal pension?

A person can make regular contributions on a monthly or annual basis or pay in a lump sum. Regular contributions can be increased. If the personal pension is a stakeholder scheme then the regular monthly contribution is limited to £20.

Limits on what can be paid in

The Inland Revenue limits the amount of tax-free contributions that can be made. Nearly everyone can contribute £3,600 per annum in total to his or her scheme. This is the before-tax-relief (gross) contribution limit. Subtracting basic tax relief makes the limit £2,808 per year. If a person is earning the contributions can be more than this.

Earnings related contributions are set as a percentage of net relevant earnings. For an employee, this means total before tax pay, including the value of most fringe benefits. If a person is self-employed, net relevant earnings means profits for tax purposes. The limits indicate the maximum before-tax-relief amount that can be paid into a personal pension plan. The table overleaf shows the percentage contribution limits. In addition to the percentages listed overleaf there is an overall cash limit on the amount of earnings which can be taken into account in working out contribution limits.

Net relevant earnings used as a basis for contributions in any particular tax year do not have to be the earnings for that particular tax year. Net relevant earnings can be chosen from any of the previous five tax years as a basis for contributions. Anyone can pay contributions on behalf of the contributor, it doesn't have to be specifically the contributor.

Tax relief on savings

A person will get tax relief up to the highest rate of income tax on the amount that is contributed to a personal pension. For example, a taxpayer paying tax at 22% can contribute £100 to a plan at a cost of only £78.

A person will get basic-rate relief automatically by paying only the after-tax relief into the plan. A person will get this relief regardless of whether they pay tax or not. For the non-taxpayer, the relief is a bonus amount paid into the plan. If a contribution is paid towards someone else's pension plan basic rate tax relief is applicable. However, for higher rate taxpayer's no extra relief can be claimed on contributions into someone else's plan.

Chapter 34

Stakeholder Pension Schemes

In April 2001 the government introduced the stakeholder pension scheme. This type of scheme is not a new plan or scheme but a set of conditions that can be applied to either personal pensions or money purchase occupational schemes. If the conditions are met then the scheme can be called a 'stakeholder pension' and will represent good value for money.

The conditions that must be met are as follows:

- The scheme will have low charges, no more than 1.5% per annum
- Low and flexible contributions. Minimum of £20 per month
- Portable-can transfer out of one scheme into another without penalty
- Simplicity-the scheme must include a default investment option which determines how money is invested if individual doesn't choose an investment option for themselves
- Information-scheme provider to give benefit statement at least once per year

If the stakeholder scheme alters then the stakeholder must be informed.
Since October 2001, employers with more than five employees who do not offer a pension arrangement must give access to a stakeholder scheme through the workplace.
All stakeholder pensions operate on a money purchase basis. Like all other money purchase schemes the pension that you will get depends on amount paid into the scheme, tax relief, charges and how well the fund does.

Chapter 35

Choosing a Personal Pension Plan

There is a wide choice of personal pension schemes on offer. One common denominator is that the schemes are now heavily regulated by both the government and the Financial Services Authority. Most schemes will accept either a monthly contribution or a one-off lump sum payment per annum. The majority of schemes will allow a person to increase contributions. It is important to look for a plan that will allow a person to miss payments, in case of unemployment, sickness etc, without penalty.

Investments
Plans which allow individuals to choose their own investments are called' Self-invested personal pensions' (SIIPS). A person will build up their own fund of personal investments from a wide range of options such as shares, gilts, property and other areas. However, unless an individual has a large sum to invest, this is unlikely to be a wise bet. Pension companies can offer their own expertise and usually have far greater knowledge than the individual.

Unit trusts and unit-linked investments
These types of plans are offered by a lot of insurance companies. The money is allocated to units whose value is linked to a specific fund of investments. The return depends on the then price of the units. Like all investments, this value will rise and fall in line with the value of the underlying investment.

Tracker funds
With a tracker fund, the main input from an investment manager is when the fund is first set up. The underlying investments are set to mimic a particular market as described by a given stock market index such as the FTSE 100. The fund is then left to track the market with no attempt being made by fund managers to switch to better markets. These types of funds do perform well and attract lower charges because of the lower input from fund managers.

With-profits plans

These types of plans are, in the main, offered by insurance companies. Money is invested in a broad spread of investments. The return depends on how well the investments grow and also the provider's profits from other parts of its business. The return is in the form of bonuses, reversionary bonuses are added to the plan regularly. A terminal bonus is normally added on redemption.

Statements are given to the pension holder showing how well the fund is doing, including an estimate of the terminal bonus. Be aware that this is only an estimate at a given time. It can rise or fall.

One disadvantage with this type of plan is that, if a person transfers their plan before it reaches maturity then any terminal bonus will be lost. Reversionary bonuses can also be lost. Therefore, when considering a with-profits plan it is very wise to read the small print.

Funds that are bond-based

Bond-based funds are a particular type of unitised fund. In this case, the underlying investments are corporate bonds, preference shares and government bonds (gilts). They are known as fixed-interest investments. A fund investing in bonds does not offer the same guaranteed returns, because fund managers will be buying and selling bonds all the time. Bonds are usually stable, particularly government bonds so the return can be expected to be stable also.

Lifestyle investments

These are quite new and the overall investment plan is designed around a persons attitude towards risk and also the planned retirement date. The earlier that a person invests the more risk that may be taken and the later that investments occur the more cautious approach that may be adopted.

Fees and other charges

Those who invest your money on your behalf don't work for nothing. Fees are charged. The rate of interest offered will reflect the ultimate charge and there will probably be an administration fee too. Some plans have very complicated charging structures and it is very important that these are understood before decisions are made.

Other benefits from a personal pension

A personal pension scheme does not automatically offer a package of benefits in addition to the actual pension. Any additional benefits have to be paid for. The range of extra benefits includes lump sum life cover for dependants if death occurs before retirement, a pension for widow or widower or other partner, a waiver of contributions if there is an inability to work and a pension paid early if sickness or disability prevents working until retirement age.

A contracted out personal pension must allow for a widows or widower's pension to be payable if the widow or widower is over 45 years of age, or is younger than 45 but qualifies for child benefit. The pension would be whatever amount can be bought by the fund built up through investing the contracting-out rebates. The widow or widower has an open market option, which gives him or her a right to shop around for a different pension provider rather than remain with the existing provider.

The pension could cease if the widow or widower remarries while under the state pension age, or ceases to be eligible for child benefit whilst still under 45. This depends on the terms of the contract at the time of death.

A contracted out widow's or widower's pension built up before 6th April 1997 must be increased each year in line with inflation, up to a maximum of 3% a year. For post April 1997 pensions this must be up to 5% per year and after 6th April 2005, pensions taken out don't have to increase at all. With the exception of contracted out plans, a person must choose at the time of taking out the plan which death benefits to have as part of the scheme. Broadly, they should be in line with the benefits mentioned above.

Retirement due to ill-health

If a person has to retire due to ill-health, a pension can be taken from a personal plan at any age. However, a person's inability to work must be clearly demonstrated and backed up with a professional opinion. Taking a pension early will result in a reduced pension because what is in the pot will be less. However, there are ways of mitigating this, one way to ensure that a waiver of premiums in the event of sickness is included in the pension. In this way the plan will continue to grow even though a person is ill. Another way is to take out permanent disability insurance. This insurance will guarantee that the pension that you will get when you cannot work will at least be a minimum amount.

Chapter 36

Transferring a Personal Pension

People will transfer a pension when they move jobs or for other reasons. However, it is always better to check all the options available before this is done.

Change of jobs

If the pension is a single lump sum or regular contribution plan then there are not usually problems with transferring. This is done simply by continuing payments into the plan with your new employer. In other words, they are fully portable. There are three exceptions to this rule:

- if a person has a contracted out personal pension for which he or she ceases to be eligible
- if a person has a non-contracted out personal pension for which he or she would cease to be eligible
- If the old employer has been paying some or all of the contributions to the personal pension. An investigation would need to be made whether the plan could continue with lower contributions or by paying in more personally

Chapter 37

Regulation of Personal Pensions

Personal pensions are covered by the investor-protection legislation embodied in the Financial Services and Markets Act 2000.

Investments are policed through a system of self-regulation. The job has been given to the Financial Services Authority, which is answerable to the Chancellor of the Exchequer. Under the current system, it is illegal for most financial firms, including pension providers, to operate in the UK unless they are authorised by the FSA or specifically exempt from authorisation.

Firms which are based outside of the UK, in another European Economic Area and subject to regulations of their own country are deemed to be authorised. There are a few exemptions from authorisation as follows:

- firms acting as agents for another firm, called 'the principal'. The principal is responsible for its agents so the principal needs to be regulated.
- Members of certain professions (lawyers, actuaries and accountants) whose investment activities are regulated by their trade body, provided that the body has been granted status as a Designated Professional Body.

The Financial Services Authority, whose address is at the back of this book, can verify the status of any company from whom a person is buying a pension.

Parliamentary Acts set out the framework of regulation, including the need for every relevant business to be authorised to carry on business in the UK. The main requirements set out:

- who is fit and proper to undertake financial business
- requirements for the business to be solvent
- how business is to be conducted

- how clients money and other assets should be handled
- what information should be disclosed to the client and in what form and frequency
- the need to keep accurate and clear record
- the need to employ compliance officers in each business
- procedures with which the regulator can check up on compliance
- complaints procedures
- disciplinary procedures

The FSA has a wide remit and does impose hefty penalties on those companies that do not comply. This is because, in the days before proper regulation, a lot of people suffered at the hands of unscrupulous firms.

The most persistent problem in recent years has been the miss-selling of personal pensions to people who might have been better off leaving their pensions where they were. As always happens when change is afoot this is exploited by the few. As a result of this problem, and high profile problems of large companies, regulation has tightened up with the result that personal pensions are quite safe.

Chapter 38

Tax and Pensions

State pensions

State retirement pensions count as income for tax purposes. Tax may have to be paid if income received is high enough. The only exception to this is the £10 Christmas bonus paid to all pensioners. State pension is paid without deduction of tax. This is convenient for non-taxpayers. For other taxpayers, the tax due will usually be deducted from PAYE or from any other pension that is received. If the tax is not deducted it will be collected through self-assessment in January and July instalments.

Occupational schemes

A pension from an occupational scheme is treated as income for tax purposes. Usually, the pension will be paid with tax deducted through the PAYE system, along with any other tax due.

Personal pensions

A personal pension will count as income for tax purposes. The pension provider will usually deduct tax through PAYE. Likewise, any other tax due will be deducted through the PAYE system. The local tax office should be contacted in order to determine individual tax positions.

Tax in retirement

When a person retires, their tax bill continues to be worked out in the usual way. However, higher tax allowances may apply so less tax is paid. The calculations used to work out a person's individual tax bill are as follows:

- income from all sources is added together. This includes all income with the exception of income that is tax-free.
- outgoings that you pay in full are deducted from taxable income. 'Outgoings' means any expenditure that qualifies for tax relief.

- allowances are subtracted. Everyone has a personal allowance. For current allowances, contact the local Inland Revenue Office or Citizens Advice Bureau. There is a breakdown below
- What is left is taxable income. This divided into three. The first slice 10% is paid (£2090) the second slice tax is paid at the basic rate (£32,400) The third slice is subject to 40% tax.
- Married couples allowance-this is a reduced rate allowance, given at a rate of 10% as a reduction to a person's tax bill. Married couples allowance is given only where a husband or wife were born before 6th April 1935.

Tax allowances for retirees

In the tax year 2006/7 the basic personal allowance for most people is £5035. However, if a person is 65 or over at any time during a tax year, there will be a higher personal allowance, the age-allowance. There are two rates of age allowance: in the 2006/7 tax year the allowance is £7280 for people reaching ages 65 to 74, and the higher age allowance is £7420 for people reaching ages 75 or more.

A husband and wife can each get a personal allowance to set against their own income. There is an extra allowance called a married couples allowance if either husband or wife, or both, were born before 6th April 1935. In 2006/7 this is £6065 if the older partner is aged up to 73 at the start of the tax year and £6135 if the older partner is aged 74 or over.

While the personal allowance saves tax at the highest rate, the married couples allowance only gives tax relief at the rate of 10% in the 2006/7tax year. If the husbands income is above a certain level then the married couples allowance is reduced, but never to less than a basic amount.

A wife can elect to have half the basic amount of the married couples allowance (but not any of the age-related addition) set against her own income. Alternatively, the husband and wife can elect jointly for the whole basic amount to be transferred to the wife.

Income limit for age allowance

Age allowances are reduced for people with earnings above a certain level. The personal age allowance is reduced if a person has a total income of more than £20,010 in the tax year 2006/7. The married couple's age allowance is also reduced if this is the case. In either case, the reduction is £1 for every £2 over the limit.

Where the husband is receiving both age-related personal allowance and age-related married couple's allowance, his personal allowance is reduced first and then the married couple's allowance. The reduction stops once the allowances fall to a basic amount.

Chapter 39

Increasing a Pension

State pension

There are a number of ways that a person may be able to increase the pension that you get from the state. If the Retirement Pension Forecast that is sent out by the Department for Work and Pensions shows that a reduced state pension is due, it may be possible to increase the amount that is received by paying voluntary Class 3 National Insurance contributions. It is possible to go back six-years to fill any gaps in a NI record.

If you go back two years, you pay contributions that applied in the earlier year. If you go back further, you will pay the rate for the year when the payment is made.

Married women's reduced rate contributions.

If a women is paying National Insurance at the married women's reduced rate, they may want to consider switching to full rate contributions instead, which will result in an increased pension. For older women, the switch to full-rate contributions generates very little extra pension. A local taxation office can advise appropriately. Leaflet CA13 National Insurance for Married Women gives details on how to make the switch.

Delaying retirement

The state pension age is currently 65 for men and 60 for women. A person can defer the date of retirement and so increase their entitlement. The whole pension must be deferred and the whole pension will benefit from the increase. Any pension for a wife based on husbands contributions must also be deferred if the husband makes this choice.

At present, it is possible to defer a pension for five years. The eventual pension will be increased by 7.5% per year if deferred. It is possible to take the increase as a lump sum, if the pension is deferred for at least a year. The amount of lump sum depends on the interest rate used by the government. The lump sum is taxable.

Occupational pension schemes

Inland Revenue rules allow a person to pay up to 15% of their earnings into a pension fund. There is a cap of £102,000. In practice, most people pay far less than this so there is a lot of room here for increasing an occupational pension. This can be achieved by paying Additional Voluntary Contributions (AVC's).

As with ordinary contributions, a person qualifies for tax-relief at the top rate of tax on the amount that is paid in AVC's. Capital gains from investing the AVC's are tax free. Part of the investment income is tax free but not income from shares, unit trusts or similar investments.

An employer who operates an in-house occupational scheme must also offer an in-house AVC scheme to enable members to make extra contributions. This scheme will normally work on a money purchase basis and money will be invested to top-up the occupational scheme. Some in-house schemes, mainly public sector schemes offer an added years AVC scheme. This is available when the main pension works on a final salary, or similar basis. Added years can be purchased from the main scheme and credited to the account of the pension holder. Another option is to pay into an independent AVC scheme offered by insurance companies and pension providers.

Personal pensions

A person can maximise the amount that they are allowed to save by making careful use of the basis-year rules. These let a person base the contributions made now on the level of earnings from any of the last five years. The year with the highest level of earnings should be chosen as the basis-year.

If a person has a retirement annuity contract there is another way to catch up on retirement savings if the full contributions limit hasn't been used up in the past few years. The carry forward rules can be used to carry forward any unused contributions relief from the last six-years. The carry forward is from the earliest tax-year first.

Combining carry-forward and carry-back rules

Carry-back and carry-forward rules can be combined, which means that a person can get unused relief from seven years ago. For example, if a contribution is made in 2006/7 it can be carried back and treated as if it was paid in 2005/6. The carry back can then be from 2000/1.

Combining carry-back and carry-forward rules can be a good idea:

- if there is a large chunk of unused tax relief in the year seven years back. If not used now it will be lost
- tax rates are lower in the current year than in the previous year and a person wants to maximise relief on large contributions
- a persons marginal rate of tax was higher in the earlier years and there is a wish to maximise relief on over-large contributions.

Personal pensions and retirement annuity contracts

A person with a retirement annuity contract can choose to make contributions to the contract, a personal pension plan or both. The choice that is made each year will affect the amount of carry-forward relief available for the retirement annuity contract.

Useful addresses and websites

The regulation of financial advice

The Financial Services Authority
25 The North Colonnade
Canary Wharf
London E14 5HS
Public enquiries helpline 0845 606 1234
www.fsa.gov.uk
Consumer helpline email:consumerhelp@fsa.gov.uk

Ombudsman
The Financial Ombudsman Service
South Quay Plaza
183 Marsh Wall
London E14 9SR
Tel: 0845 080 1800
www.financial-ombudsman.org.uk

The above deals with complaints about individual pensions and free standing AVC's, life insurance, general insurance and investment products.

Other ombudsmen, complaints and advice schemes
The Pensions Ombudsman
11 Belgrave Road
London SW1V 1RB
020 7834 9144
www.pensions-ombudsman.org.uk
The above deals with complaints about occupational pension schemes.

The Office for the Pensions Advisory Service Opas
11 Belgrave Road
London SW1V 1RB
020 7233 8080

www.opas.org.uk

For advice about occupational and personal pension schemes.

The Occupational Pensions Regulatory Authority (Opra)
Invicta House
Trafalgar Place
Brighton BN1 4DW
001273 627600

www.opra.gov.uk
www.stakeholder.opra.gov.uk
For general complaints about the running of company pension schemes.

The Office for the Supervision of Solicitors
Victoria Court
8 Dormer Place
Leamington Spa
Warwick CV32 5AE
01926 822007

The Ombudsman for Estate Agents
Beckett House
4 Bridge Street
Salisbury Wilts SP1 2LX
01722 333306

The Mortgage Code Arbitration Scheme
11 Bloomsbury Square
London WC1A 2LT
020 7421 7444

The General Insurance Standards Council
110 Cannon Street
London EC4N 6EU
0845 601 2857
www.gisc.co.uk

Pensions and retirement

The Pension Schemes Registry
PO Box 1NN
Newcastle under Tyne
NE9 1N
0191 225 6316

To track down old company pension schemes

The Pre-retirement Association
9 Chesham Road
Guildford
Surrey GU1 3LS
01483 301170
www.pra.uk.com

The Pensions Compensation Board
11 Belgrave Road
London SW1V 1RB
020 7828 9794

Financial Advisers
IFA Promotion
17-19 Emery Road
Brislington
Bristol BS4 5PF
0800 085 3250

www.ifap.org.uk

The Money Management Directory of fee based Advisers
C/O Matrix Data Services
Freepost 22
London W1E 1BR
0870 013 1925
www.uk/fadirectory.co.uk

The Association of Private Client Investment managers and Stockbrokers (APCIMS)
112 Middlesex Street
London E1 7HY
020 7247 70870

www.apcims.co.uk

The Society of Financial Advisers (Sofa)
20 Aldermanbury
London EC2V 7HY
020 7417 4442

www.sofa.org

The Association of Solicitor Investment managers (ASIM)
Chiddingstone Causeway
Tonbridge
Kent TN11 8JX
01892 870065

www.asim.org.uk

Solicitors for Independent Advice4
10 East Street
Epsom
Surrey KT17 1HH
01372 721172

www.solicitor-ifa.co.uk

The Association of Pension Lawyers
C/O Pinsent Curtis Biddle
1 Gresham Street
London EC2V 7BU
020 7418 700
www.apl.org.uk

The Ethical Investment Research Service
80-84 Bondway
London SW8 1SF
0845 606 0324

www.eiris.org

Accountants

The Institute of Chartered Accountants in England and Wales
Moorgate Place
London EC2P 2BJ
020 7920 8100

www.icaew.co.uk

The Institute of Chartered Accountants in Scotland
21 Haymarket Yards
Edinburgh EH12 5BH
0131 347 0100

www.icas.org.uk

The Association of Chartered Certified Accountants
29 Lincoln's In Fields
London WC2A 3EE
020 7396 7000

www.accaglobal.com

The Chartered Institute of Taxation and The Association of Tax Technicians
12 Upper Belgrave Street
London SW1X 8B
020 7235 9381

www.tax.org.uk

Specialist Magazines

Money Management
3rd Floor
Maple House
149 Tottenham Court Road
London W1P 9LL
020 7896 2525

Planned Savings
6-77 Paul Street
London EC2A 4LG
020 753 1000
Money management and Planned Savings are aimed at professional advisers.

Moneyfacts
Moneyfacts House
6-70 Thorpe Road
Norwich NR1 1BJ
01603 476476

www.moneyfacts.co.uk

This magazine publishes a monthly round up of all savings account rates. For more up-to-date listings see the web site.

Trade Bodies

The Association of Investment Trust Companies
Durrant House
8-13 Chiswell Street
London EC21Y 4YY
0800 085 8520
www.itsonline.co.uk www.aitc.co.uk

Provides information on aspects of investing in investment trust companies.

The Investment Management Association

65 Kingsway
London WC2B 6TD
020 8207 1361
www.investmentuk.org
Provides information on investing in unit trusts and Oeics

Proshare
Centurion House
24 Monument Street
London EC2R 8AQ
020 7394 5200

www.proshare.org.uk
Advises on setting up investment clubs and runs education programmes for schools on share ownership

The Association of British Insurers
61 Gresham Street
London EC2V 7HQ
020 7600 333

www.abi.org.uk
Publishes information sheets on all aspects of insurance.

The British Insurance Brokers Association
14 Bevis Marks
London EC3A 7NT
020 7623 9043

www.biba.org.uk

The Building Societies Association
3 Savile Row
London W1S 3PB
020 7437 0655
www.bsa.org.uk
The Council of Mortgage Lenders

3 Savile Row
London W1S 3BP
020 7437 0655

The National Association of Estate Agents
Arbon House
21 Jury Street
Warwick CV34 4EH
01926 496800
www.naea.co.uk

The Royal Institution of Chartered Surveyors
12 Great George Street
Parliament Square
London SW1P 3AD
020 7222 7000
www.rics.org.uk

The Association of Residential Letting Agents
Maple House
53-5 Woodside Road
Amersham
Bucks HP6 6AA
01923 89655
www.aria.co.uk

Borrowing
The National Debtline
0808 808 4000

The Association of British Credit Unions
Holyoake House
Hanover Street
Manchester M60 OAS
0161 832 8694
www.abcul.org

Credit Information Agencies
Experian
Consumer help services
PO Box 8000
Nottingham NG1 5GX
0870 241 6212

www.experian.com

Equifax Europe (UK)
Credit file advice centre
PO Box 3001
Glasgow G81 0583
0870 010 0583
www.equifax.co.uk

Investment information websites

www.investment-gateway.com
www.new-online-investor.co.uk
www.find.co.uk